Grandpa Still Remembers

*Life changing stories
for kids of all ages
from a missionary kid
in Africa*

Paul Brown

Illustrated by

Deborah Joy Brown Armes

Torchflame Books
An imprint of Light Messages

Copyright © 2013, by Paul Brown.
Grandpa Still Remembers
Life changing stories for kids of all ages
from a missionary kid in Africa
Paul Brown
p.brown13468@gmail.com
www.missionarystories.net

Torchflame Books
An imprint of Light Messages Publishers
Durham, North Carolina
Printed in the United States of America
ISBN: 978-1-61153-027-8

To my dear wife

Ellen

Without whom there would have been no grandchildren

And to

Rethy

Our fifteenth grandchild

These are just some simple stories grandpa still remembers from his life at Rethy, maybe because he learned something from them. I just wanted to share them with you. You might like to share them with your friends.

With love,

Grandpa Paul

The cover picture, a Zande man in a dugout canoe, was taken on the Uele River near the place where we found the Bac sunk in the river when we left for boarding school at 2:00 a.m. We were headed up river on an early morning hippo hunt.

Contents

To Help You Understand

Maybe you don't know much about your grandpa, and that doesn't matter; but if you wonder why his stories are so different, it's because he grew up at a boarding school in Africa. He doesn't remember what happened before his dad, your great-grandpa, went to the Belgian Congo to start his own hospital in a remote area among the Zande people. You see your great-grandpa was a doctor and your great-grandma was a nurse. They wanted to go live at Banda and help the people who had no doctor. For over a hundred miles in any direction there was no help for the Zandes when they got sick, except for their own powerful medicine men that we called witch doctors.

The witch doctors had some medicines from roots, bark, plants, and leaves, but lots of the time they could do nothing to heal the sick person. They made little bags of spirit medicine to conceal under the patient's cloths. The bag hung by a thin thong of leather around the patient's neck. It was to help him get well. There could be some parts of a dead bird like feathers, claws or bones, and maybe some pebbles and other tiny mysterious objects inside the bag.

To communicate with the spirits, the witch doctors would rub the two parts of their worn communications board together as they chanted, waiting for the parts to stick. Maybe they would poison a chicken and do a ceremony while watching to see when it would die. This was to figure out who had placed a curse on the person to make them sick. Maybe the Ouija board would stick or the poisoned chicken would die while he chanted the name of one of the sick person's enemies. The witch doctors put curses on other people, too, if they got paid a goat or a chicken. You see, the Zandes worshiped the spirits, and they didn't know about Jesus. To tell them what Jesus did for them was the main reason my mom and dad went to Africa.

I started boarding school when I was just five years old. Boarding school is where you stay all the time and live in a dormitory with other kids. You do everything together, not just school work. Since my parents lived at Banda, 550 miles away from Rethy, I didn't see them very often: sometimes not until vacation time after three months at school. Lots of things happen at boarding schools that don't happen at home to other kids. I'll tell you what I still remember. The people I talk about are real people, and I want them to forgive me if they don't remember things just the same way I do. You see, I'm not so young anymore, and I forget too.

Of course your grandpa grew up and fell in love with your grandma. I could tell you some of those stories too, but not all of them. Grandpa and Grandma went back to Africa and worked for a long time at Rethy, right where I went to school. You see we wanted to tell people about Jesus and started by being dorm parents for 23 boys and girls before your mom or dad was even born. We had lots of fun with our borrowed kids. They became like our kids too; we loved them so much.

I wasn't always a teacher and a dorm parent. I got to build lots of things, from a well in the marsh to a radio tower in the sky. To make electricity, I worked on a big dam on a river at the top of a hill to collect the water to run a turbine and 400 KVA generator installed partway down the hill. I was made the director of Editions CECA where we had lots of workers, some of whom ran big printing presses that sometimes needed fixing.

Now I'm trying farming on our small family farm in New York and using computers to do accounting, e-mail, and other work for our North Africa tour business. I'm making a little book for you too. Rethy's mom, Debbie Armes, drew all the pictures for the beginning of each chapter.

I hope you like the book.

Love,

Grandpa Paul

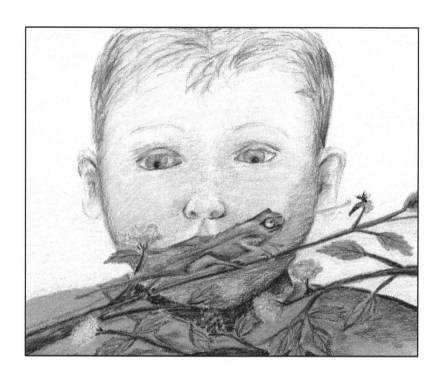

Too Small

When I was little, I wanted to be a Titchie at Rethy Academy, a boarding school for missionary kids in the Belgian Congo. The school was at Rethy, the same place we lived when my mom and dad first went to Africa to be missionaries. My mom and dad worked at the hospital to learn more about the weird diseases that exist in Africa. Since the school was a long ways away, on top of the next hill more than a mile away, I had to stay at home.

At a boarding school you get to go away from home to live with the other kids all the time. You get to eat there too. You even get to sleep there. You don't have to come home at night. I think you have to go to school, but you don't have to ask your mom for permission to go to the dorm to play.

My mom later told me that I was so eager to go that I even packed my cardboard suitcase and told her that I was all ready.

She said, "I don't think so. You are just five years old and too small to go away from home."

I wasn't so small. I was big enough to go hunting for birds with my bow and arrow. I had a special arrow. On the four-pointed tip of the arrow there was sticky gray stuff from the sap of the big old rubber tree behind the hospital. My little friend told me it was the very best arrow for shooting birds. The man who made it for me wrapped the split head with sisal string covered with sticky, cooked sap from that tree to make it strong and four times as good at getting birds. It would stick to the bird, and I might even get a pet bird. I might hit a bird in the tail making it unable to fly away carrying that heavy arrow. It would grow new tail feathers and be my very own pet.

I don't think I ever did hit a bird, but I did lots of sneaking around, half crouched, my arrow ready on the string of my little bow. Black and white birds, called Wagtails, would keep running ahead of me then fly a little way, land, and bob their tails up and down. I don't think my mom would be happy to know that I was hunting Wagtails. She had said, "They are such friendly birds. Don't bother them." Because they were the easiest ones to sneak up on, I spent hours trying to shoot one. My arrow lost all its stickiness since it hit the dirt so often, but I didn't lose it for a long time. I never did get a Wagtail that I can remember.

STILL
TOO SMALL

I do remember that I was able to find chameleons. I would look for a long time on the hedge that had the fuzzy leaves, the tiny bunches of colored flowers, and the little clumps of green berries. The green berries would grow as big as BBs and eventually turn black. Some of the kids ate them, but I didn't. When the berries were black, I think the chameleons found more insects on those Lantana hedges. Chameleons were hard to find since they would stay completely still and make themselves the same shade of green as the hedge. The patterns on their backs and the patterns made by the twigs and leaves looked just the same. The hedge was the best place to look for chameleons.

I would stand very still for a long time, and sometimes a chameleon would move; then I would finally see him. They have skinny legs and feet sort of like mittens with no separate toes. The tiny claws, two on one side and three on the other side, help them clamp onto the branch they are climbing. Chameleons move the front foot on one side and the back foot on the other side at the same time, little by little, until each foot reaches the new place on which to hold. They feel around with their feet for the best spot and don't even look. Then, they move the other two feet.

When chameleons sneak up on a fly, their tails stick out straight behind them, not touching anything. They advance bit by bit, maybe when they think the fly isn't looking. Their eyes bulge way out on both sides of their head. Wrinkly skin covers the entire eye except the tiny hole in the center where they can see. Their eyes roll around and around to look in front, in back, sideways, and up and down. Each one goes a different way until they are ready to catch a fly.

The chameleon I had been watching stopped. Both eyes checked all around again, but then they came together, almost cross-eyed, both focusing directly on a small fly. The layered skin under the chameleon's chin started bulging out bigger and bigger. His mouth turned up almost like a smile opening just a little crack.

Suddenly, so fast I would have missed it if I hadn't been concentrating, the chameleon's long tongue shot out and the end stuck to the fly. The tongue was even longer than the chameleon. Chameleons almost never miss. His long tongue quickly disappeared, curling up somewhere inside as he pulled the fly into his grinning mouth. Once again his eyes began searching around and around in different directions. He chewed very slowly.

I grabbed for him. He couldn't move very quickly, though he tried to get away. He might have dropped off the branch down into the bush and then it would have been nearly impossible to find him again. I caught him around his fat middle. He tried to bite, but the rough edge of his mouth wasn't very sharp, and his mouth was smaller than my fingertip. Some chameleons hiss too. Even though my little friend was scared of them, *I wasn't*. Chameleons have bad spirits in them he told me, but I didn't believe it. The chameleon knew he was caught, or maybe he wasn't so scared because after a little while he stopped squirming.

When I freed him, he started walking across my hand. He might have wanted to walk off, but I kept on putting the other hand in front so that he never got to the edge. He slowed down. He stopped. He sat there on my thumb, looking round and round with his bulging, wandering eyes. He slowly turned a dull black and his markings got blurred. He curled his tail and became very still. He liked my warm little thumb, I think. I finally had a pet.

I kept him in my window on the curtain, but he didn't turn red. He got sort of brown. I caught flies for him in some of the other windows, but he didn't seem hungry any more. I got tired of watching him. After dinner, I proudly showed him to my mom, but she said, "I don't want him in the house. He might go walking on the floor and someone might step on him and squash him."

"If he is a mother he could have tiny little chameleons," I told her, "lots of them. They would be just this big! Wouldn't that be neat?"

"You better let him go," she said. I don't think she thought it would be easy *not* to step on all those little chameleons. I took him outside and put him on a rosebush in my mother's rose garden, but he got lost.

I thought I was big enough to go to boarding school, but I still had to get big. I guess you need to be pretty big to do lots of things, but I remembered the story my Mom read that night from the Bible. She said, "Little children are never too small to come to Jesus."

The people in the story were telling the children not to bother Jesus. I think my mom thought I was a bother sometimes because she would tell me to go outside to play and let her do her work.

Mom read in the story where Jesus said, "Let the little children to come to Me; do not hinder *them*, for to such belongs the kingdom of God. Truly I say to you, whoever does not receive the kingdom of God like a little child, he shall not enter into it."

Mom said, "That means to let the little children come because He loves them." I liked that. She said, "Jesus likes people to be like little children when they come to Him because they believe everything He says, and they know He can take care of anything."

I was glad I wasn't too small to come to Jesus. I could find another chameleon tomorrow. Jesus would help me find one.

The Bible story is in Mark 10:13-16

Running Away

Before I was six, I did get to go to boarding school. My mom put nametags on all my clothes for someone else to read at a place called the laundry. There was a list inside my suitcase, too, to help me not lose anything, I think. She would know what I had lost when I came home after three months. I even got to live in the dorm.

There were five boys my age and a few girls in the other dorm, but girls didn't count much then. My bed was the top bunk bed, and I could look out the window. Gary Kline's bed was underneath mine, and he used to try to dump me off by pushing up on the leather straps that held up my thin mattress. Peter Epp and Kenny Schuit slept in the other double bunk bed. Lester Harris had the single bed. Mr. Schuit was our dorm parent, and he woke us up every morning with a bell.

Miss Stewart was our teacher, and she knew everything. She even knew we needed to run outside sometimes, "to get out the wiggles." She talked about stick medicine. When we were disobedient, we learned what it was, but she let us sit on her lap when we read stories together. Mr. Miller was the principal. I think he was in charge of everybody. I liked it at Rethy Academy.

Gary broke his arm, and he got a white cast on it. Lester told lots of stories about hunting birds. Kenny was best friends with Peter. He collected stamps. Peter collected the birds' eggs we found. He poked a little hole in one end of the egg with a needle. He made a little bigger hole in the other end and poked the needle all around inside the egg to break the yoke then blew gently on the small hole until all the slimy inside stuff came out of the egg. Then he put it on cotton in a box. Lester knew what kind of bird laid the egg by the pattern on the eggshell or by the shape of the nest. I watched quietly from my top bunk bed and wished I could find another chameleon.

Peter was the one with lots of ideas. Soon they were talking about running away from school. They took bread from the dining hall for their trip. It was hard to tell how many slices of bread they took since each slice was smashed into their pockets and broke into smaller pieces as they took them out to put into the pillowcase from Kenny's bed. They added some green guavas and blood oranges from the orchard. Sometimes the guavas were quite good if they were pink inside, even though they were tiny and green outside. We were always in the orchard looking for guavas at recess time, so it was hard to find any pink ones. I thought the guavas in the pillowcase looked like they might still be white inside. They decided that they would run away on Saturday, *really* early in the morning.

Saturday, before I could even see the sun out of my window, I felt the bed shaking. Gary was trying to get dressed. He was having a hard time getting his shirt on because the sling for his cast got in the way. Peter and Lester got dressed quickly.

Kenny did too. I lay on my tummy with my pillow wadded up under my chin. I watched from my top bunk. Gary wanted them to help him, but they ignored him. His shirt kept getting stuck on his cast. He couldn't bend that arm behind him very well even when he took off the sling. He was still asking for help when they put on their jackets, picked up the lumpy pillowcase, and snuck out the door. There was some whispering in the hall. Some other boys joined them.

Gary tried really hard to get ready. In the end his shirt wasn't on right, and the buttons weren't closed. He put on his jacket the best he could and went out the door to try to catch up with them. After a few minutes, he came back. They were gone. A little while later Mr. Schuit came down the hall ringing the bell. It was time to wake up and have devotions.

I don't know how the dorm parents found out. Adults don't tell you what they are doing. I didn't find out for a long time where they went or how far they got. I don't know why they decided to run away. I never wondered why I wasn't asked to join them. I didn't feel like running away anyway.

Lester Harris is now a missionary, and he once was telling stories about that time. They had walked what seemed to them like a long, long time and almost got to the press at Rethy. The press is almost a mile from the dorm if you follow the road. If you sneak through the deep valley, through the marsh, through the thorn bushes and the black wattle forest, it is still almost a mile. The Congolese probably told the missionaries at Rethy which way the little band of runaway boys had gone. They were found near the Cook's house, still on Rethy Station and very tired from their adventure.

Did running away help anything? They didn't even get very far. I don't know if they finished their smashed bread and green guavas, but they did miss breakfast.

On Monday, Miss Stewart told us lots about running away, stealing time and stuff, but I was only partly listening. There was a Wagtail on the steps. I think he was trying to catch flies in that sunny spot. There was a good Bible story about it too.

"A man called Jonah tried to run away," Miss Stewart said. " But God sent a storm to stop the ship. Then, when the sailors threw him into the sea to stop the storm, God sent a big fish to carry him back to where he was supposed to be. God had something for Jonah to do and a lesson to teach Jonah."

Have you ever wanted to run away?

It is much better to do what God says. He loves you. Won't He give you what you need each day? Sure He will. He likes to be with you. He said, "Have I not commanded you? Be strong and courageous. Do not be frightened, and do not be dismayed, for Jehovah your God *is* with you wherever you go."

Can you run away from what God wants you to do? I guess you can try, but it won't do any good.

The Bible story is in the book of Jonah

Leaving for School at 2 a.m.

We were going to go back to school from Banda to Rethy all in one day. I'm sure I wasn't any help in the preparations.

Dad went to the hospital to operate; that's what he always did. Mom was usually over there, too, while I played with my sister, Winnie. We tried to get birds with the slingshot wrapped with red bicycle inner tube that our cook had made for me. We looked for birds' eggs. We dreamed up ways to trap birds, but never succeeded. They never went under the box. We tracked animals; cows were the easiest. My little brother, Timmy, was only four and not much good at hunting birds. My older sister was always trying to draw pictures of sunsets. She got to drink tea and coffee and always used big words like "condiments." My favorite sister, Winnie, and I called her "Coffee, tea, comments."

Mom had had me try on all these clothes for school and seemed pleased when they were too big. She wouldn't even pack my favorite stuff. She sewed nametags on everything, even my laundry bag. My big sister helped her, I guess. There was a list taped to the top of my trunk again of all the stuff Mom put inside. She put two oatmeal tins in my trunk too, one full of peanut butter cookies. She sealed up the other tin with lots of surgical tape. It had peanut butter in it.

My mom gave me a haircut with the shiny clippers. She had to squeeze and squeeze to make the little cutters move from side to side to cut my hair. If she didn't squeeze often enough as she went up the back of my head, she pulled out the hair instead of cutting it. She missed some near the top of my ear, but she also missed my ear.

My trunk was already loaded into the back of the Dix's Chevrolet truck with all the other stuff to get ready to leave early tomorrow. Betty Lou Pierson had come down from Asa with her dad. Tomorrow we were all going to drive to Rethy in the Dix's truck, more than 550 miles one way. I thought Carol Dix was pretty; Minnie Mae always seemed to be happy, and Richard used to beat me up. I don't think he really tried to hurt me. Since we wouldn't have to stop at Dungu this time for the Weiss boys, I heard that we could go all the way to Rethy in one day if we started at 2:00 a.m.

It would be neat if I could get a place near the front of the truck, on top of the load, overlooking the faded green, dented, rusty cab, but the big kids would take all the best spots. I found a hollow near the front corner where I could burrow down and hide from the night wind but still look out through the slats of the truck back. Nobody seemed to mind when I sat in the little hole wishing for tomorrow to come while they finished packing the truck and filling it with gas.

I watched them fill the gas tank through a yellow plastic hose. Mr. Dix's old felt hat was laid out inside the tin funnel to filter the gas that came down through the hose from the jerry tin the man held up on top of the cab. More gas was in the drum under the load since there was no place to get it until we got to Dungu. Maybe that gas would be too expensive, or there might not even be any.

That night I crawled under my covers completely dressed except for my shoes. Maybe Mom noticed, or maybe she just understood that I wanted to be all ready to go.

Only minutes after my Mom woke me up, I was at the door waiting for my sister. I stood there shining my flashlight all around, looking at the big night blooming flowers lining our front path. The night air smelled of the perfume of the frangipani tree flowers. I could see flashlights over at Dixes' where the truck was waiting. My sister was still brushing her teeth. Mom made me go back and get my coat, but I didn't really need it. I think she gave me a kiss; Dad said goodbye. Parents do that, but I was in a hurry to get to my spot on the truck.

It seemed like a long time before we started down Banda hill on the winding gravel road under the mango trees. I could smell the rotting mangos. The tires crunched on the ironstone gravel. The shining red eyes of the night birds winked out when they flew silently off the road. We got to the leprosy camp where Dad treated lots of people, but no one was moving around. We turned right and started on the Niangara road. It had two pontoons to cross the rivers but was lots shorter than the Doruma road.

The truck started going faster and faster. Even though I squinted my eyes, it was still hard to look into the wind. I was looking for night birds and maybe elephants. Tears blew back along my cheeks.

The big kids were trying to catch the night birds that must have felt trapped in the brilliant beam of light from the headlights of the truck. They have great big eyes in order to see the bugs at night in the dim light of the moon. Long before we got close enough to see the birds, we saw the little red dots of light their eyes reflected from the truck's headlights. Usually the tiny dot just vanished. Most of them flew away before we got very close. Some stayed in the road until we could even see the shadow behind them. They looked just like the road until they flew up; some to one side, some to the other as they disappeared into the black night. Some flew up too late and there was a soft thump when the truck hit them. The big kids were waiting for one to fly up high enough to miss the truck but still be in their reach as they stood on top of the load. Since they had to hold on too, they didn't have much success. I remember Paul Lindquist once caught one, but it got away when his brother Don pulled open the wings to see the pattern on the feathers. I liked the Pennant Winged Nightjars the best. I hoped they'd catch one, but I was getting cold just watching.

I buttoned the top button of my coat. Moms are pretty smart. I was so cold. I burrowed further down into my little hole and watched the tall elephant grass swish by in a blur beside the truck. Mr. Dix knew the way. He was a good driver. I guessed I didn't have to watch out for elephants. Down in my little hole, out of the wind, it was a little warmer. The tires made a buzzing sound on the gravel. The canvas smelled funny.

We had started on the long trip to Rethy, and I wouldn't see my mom and dad for the next three months. I was going to live in the dorm again and go to school, but I wasn't worried about anything, even though I knew so little of what was ahead of me.

THE "BAC" MADE
OF DUGOUT CANOES, LOGS & PLANKS

I really didn't even know how long three months was. I was getting as warm as I could in my little hole amidst the duffle bags and trunks under the edge of the canvas. The truck drove on into the black night.

I remembered another story Miss Stewart told us about a man who was supposed to leave his home and all his family and go to a new country far away. He was told that this new country would be for all his kids and their kids. They would be as many as the stars in the sky.

I knew I was going to Rethy, and I knew we would cross the Bac on the way. I knew I would find my friends and Miss Stewart at Rethy when we arrived. The man in the Bible started off his journey to a new country he had never seen and knew nothing about! "By faith Abraham obeyed when he was called to go out to a place that he was to receive as an inheritance. And he went out, not knowing where he was going."

He didn't even know the way there. He believed he would have lots of descendants, too, even though he was 75 years old, his wife was 65, and they didn't have even one kid! I didn't know a grandma and grandpa could have kids when they got that old!

That was because God was the One who told him to go, and he believed what God said. God liked that, so he called Abraham His friend.

The Bible story is in Genesis 12:1-9

The Sunken Bac

We were stopped. It was quiet. My nose was cold. I covered it with my warm hand. The big kids weren't on the truck.

When I looked out over the truck cab, I saw the headlights shining into the dark where the road went down into the swirling black water of the Uele River. Two big partly submerged planks marked the end of the road where it disappeared into the water. The big kids looked white in the glare of the headlights. They were standing at the river's edge, looking towards the middle of the river. The far bank was hard to see in the dark. I heard a two-tone Zande goo-goo drum beating out a sound pattern that repeated over and over; then it stopped. We were at the first pontoon.

Mr. Dix was talking Pazande to a man who just stood there and listened. He had his arms folded across his naked chest with his hands tucked into his armpits. He didn't seem to be agreeing with Mr. Dix, and he looked like he wanted to go back to his smoky lean-to with the orange, flickering firelight that he had just left. The headlights made it easy to see the holes in his pants. They were all fuzzy around the edges.

"Ay-ee Ba, ako Ba, si rengbhe nga te," he said. After a while he said, "ee Ba, ee Ba, ah-ne sude-he, wo du."

He had changed from saying, "No sir. Sorry sir. It can't be done," to, "Yes sir. Yes sir. We'll try; yes you are right."

The drum was beating again, with a different sound pattern. Almost at once there was faint shouting from the dark on the other side of the river along with clunking and splashing sounds. The men who had been summoned were coming across in a dugout canoe. Mr. Dix came back to the truck and started the motor, leaving it idle to charge the battery so he could keep the headlights shining out over the darkly flowing water.

I climbed out of my warm little hole on the back of the truck and went to stand near my big sister at the edge of the river. I could see flashing reflections of light on the swirling water and something dark sticking up, some logs or something. My sister told me that the Bac was stuck in the middle of the river on a sand bar.

Bac is the French name for what we called the pontoon boat, a floating raft made of huge mahogany boards attached across about eight or ten big dugout canoes. The boards were spaced as far apart as the wheels of a truck and nearly twice as long as the truck. The men used long poles, which they lowered between the canoes to push on the river bottom. They pushed and walked to the end of the canoe to make the pontoon move. Near the middle of the river the whole pole could be under water if it was rainy season, then for a while they had to paddle. They would first pole the pontoon upstream before they started across because they drifted downstream again when they paddled.

To get up onto the pontoon, the truck was to be driven up a ramp made from the big planks that now lay partly in the water at the river's edge. They would lift the planks into place, then drop a big long bolt into the hole in the plank and on the pontoon boat. That held everything in place while the truck was driven up. Mr. Dix had to drive quickly up the wet planks because they were so slippery, but he always stopped right in the middle of the pontoon so it would be level. I liked the pontoons. There were usually frogs in the water that leaked into the huge dugout canoes. When the truck was driven on the pontoon, the water would leak in faster under the little tin plates that covered the holes in the dugout canoes. Even though there were lots of nails around the edges, the patches still leaked. Today it was still dark. Maybe it wouldn't be so much fun, especially since the pontoon was stuck out there on the sandbar.

Mr. Dix went out in a dugout canoe to the sandbar. He was out in the middle of the river for a long time with those men who had come when the drum called. You could easily see him working with the men. He was the biggest, and his shirt was white. They were struggling with poles and things trying to move the Bac.

The sky started to get a little lighter. The big kids had been playing tag, mostly in the light in front of the truck, but now they chased each other up the road.

I discovered a Zande bird trap. It had a circle of short sticks holding a Zande-made string about an inch above the ground. The string had an open slip-knot

ZANDE
BAKBKE
TRAP

with the middle tied to a short, lever stick placed under a strong, forked stake driven into the ground. The other end of the slipknot was anchored to the ground. The lever was held in place since the bent spring stick pulled up on one end while the other end was propped up onto the top of the upright trigger stick. The trigger stick was stuck through a piece of meat. If something grabbed the meat, it was easy to see that the trigger stick would move and the short, lever stick on the string would slip out from under the forked stake. The bent down spring stick would snap up and close the slipknot tightly against the forked stake.

"It is for a Ba-Kee-Kee," the pontoon guard man told me. Those are the brown hawks that can swoop down and snatch things off the ground, then eat as they fly. The Zande trap was a lot better than Winnie's and my box trap with the prop-stick and long string.

The birds were starting to wake up. It was almost daylight. The big kids were calling me. They were already on top of the truck. I looked at the pontoon, mostly under the water, still in the middle of the river. The black water now looked brown, except for the white little waves and bubbles slipping downstream around the sunken Bac.

We drove all the way back up the hill to Banda before we started the second time on our trip to Rethy. They had to put more gas in the truck to replace all we had used. "We have to go the Doruma road," Mr. Dix said. He sent my big sister and me to say goodbye to Mom and Dad again; I think so Mr. Dix could say hi to his wife and maybe get some dry cloths. He liked his wife. I could tell.

Would you like to go away to boarding school, in Africa, for three months by truck, starting out at 2:00 in the morning? I was an MK, a third culture kid. Some people say that going to a boarding school like we did is bad. They say we don't fit in with the other kids. We have no idea what is most important to other kids our age in our home culture. We don't even talk like them.

Jesus was definitely from a different culture, despised more than anybody else. "Marvel not if the world hates you," Jesus said. "You are not of this world, even as I am not of this world."

It is good to love Jesus first, and it doesn't really matter if other kids who hate Him don't think you are cool. What God gives you in this life is the very best for you. If you are doing what He wants you to do, then the experiences are meant for you. I enjoyed growing up in Africa, as the son of missionaries. To love Jesus first is the very best thing.

The Bible story is in Daniel chapter 6.

Poor Billy Deans

I remember Billy Deans. He wasn't very big nor was I. We both lived in the dorm at Rethy.

I remember kids saying my ears were big and my knees were double jointed. It was Andy Englebreck who hit the back of my knees and laughed when they sort of snapped forward. The other boys laughed with him. Since they were all bigger than I was, I just stood there when they banged the back of my knees again and went off laughing. Andy had a big kneecap that stuck out in front, and his legs weren't very straight. He had much bigger ears than I did, much, much bigger. But he was bigger too, so I never wore shorts again. They didn't "bonk" my knees any more. They had more important things to do, like picking on Billy Deans.

I don't remember if Billy had big ears, but his legs were fine as far as I know. I think his nose was pretty straight too, not like mine, which turned up a little at the end. I used to try to see if I could make it straight, checking cross-eyed to see if it worked. My nose didn't attract much attention because David's nose was different, really different. The end was somehow too short or not there, and his nostrils were round holes. The boys would push the top of their noses way back, wrinkle their face, snuff in and out, and then laugh. I felt sorry for David, but didn't dare tell them they looked stupid doing that and that David couldn't help it. There was nothing wrong with Billy's nose that I can remember, but Billy ran away.

Billy had a different problem. He was too big to wet his bed, but he still did. Billy would try to make his bed really quickly so no one would find out, but after a couple of days it would be stinky. His PJ's were stinky too. The alarm clock his parents gave him didn't wake him up. I don't remember hearing it. I guess we were all sound asleep. His parents gave him something else too so he would wake up. It was two thin tin foil pads with a sheet of dry tissue in between. I don't know how it was supposed to work, but if it got wet it was supposed to wake up Billy. It didn't. Poor guy.

The dorm parents tried all sorts of things. Of course he couldn't drink anything at supper. I think he even got spankings to make him try harder not to wet his bed. We were even told not to play with Billy until he grew up and didn't wet his bed. He didn't smell too good,

HOT BATH WATER

so no one played with him anyway.

Sometimes he smelled so bad he had to have a bath when it wasn't even bath day. The water was only hot on bath day. They used to make hot water for baths by building a wood fire under the half drum outside. We carried it in buckets from the drum outside and poured it into the old wooden bathtub, but we couldn't waste wood and water to have hot baths every day. The water had to be carried up from the covered spring hole in the valley, four barrels at a time in the old ox cart.

Billy had to wash his sheets every time he got caught, and he could be found nearly every day at recess quietly scrubbing his sheets in the bathtub. Of course we yelled at him to rinse the tub and not dribble the water on the floor when he carried the sheets out to the clothesline. He didn't have any friends. He wasn't very happy. Maybe the only time he could relax was when he was asleep. We went our own way and didn't think about Billy very much.

One time, on April Fool's Day, our new dorm parent, Mr. Stauffacher, came down the hall to wake us up. He was pretending to be angry that we were so slow in waking up. Actually, we had decided to play a trick on him and had balanced a plastic cup half full of water on top of the partly open door to our hall. Hiding behind our doors, wide-awake, we looked through the cracks, waiting to see what would happen. He slammed the door open, got soaked down the front of his green khaki work cloths, and began laughing. He was really a pretty patient guy. Then we told him that Deans had wet his bed.

He went in to check. None of us had checked, but the guy with the idea to tattle on Billy was right. Poor guy. The dorm parent told him to get out of bed, wash his sheets, and take a bath. It was almost like routine. He wasn't even mad. Billy didn't say much, but just went down the hall hugging his smelly sheets on the way to the bathroom. We had also gotten used to Billy's problem, but Billy was never included in anything.

When we got up one morning, Billy was gone. No one had any idea when he had left or where he might have gone. We were scared to tell the dorm parent. It seemed like no one cared, except the dorm parent. He was really concerned.

We were sent to school like usual, and everyone who wasn't teaching was looking for Billy. All the workmen were looking for Billy. Hours went by. Now there is no way a little white missionary's kid could disappear in a world of black people. Everybody would notice him, but no one had seen him. The workers were worried too. I think they loved us more than we understood, and soon lots of local people, even people from the Dukas, were looking for Billy. Where could he have gone? It was nearly time for lunch. It started raining, like it often did just before noon. Then it began raining so hard we couldn't even see across the valley to the press. The teachers wouldn't let us go to the dorm until it let up a little. Finally, it slowed down a little, and we ran to dinner.

We followed the normal schedule. We had lunch. The dish crew did their job. The table setting crew set the tables for supper. The adults, however, were talking to each other trying to decide what to do next, I guess. They might have radioed to the Deans that they couldn't find their son. It kept raining, but not quite so hard. The water running down the gutters to the cistern wasn't spilling over onto the path any more. We ran back to school through the drizzling rain and didn't even get scolded for forgetting our raincoats and boots.

By nighttime, we knew they had found him.

Why did Billy run away? Did he think nobody loved him? Did he think nobody cared? Was he happy? What was he thinking about? Nobody told us exactly why he ran away, but it isn't too hard to guess is it?

The Bible says to be kind one to another, to love one another, to carry each other's burdens. "We who are strong have an obligation to bear with the failings of the weak, and not to please ourselves." It says lots of things that we need to add to our faith, and at the end of the list it says to add to our brotherly kindness, love. Had we shown love to Billy? No, we hadn't even been kind, certainly not tenderhearted, and he had run away.

Nobody knew what Billy's plan was, but he wasn't found for a whole day, even with lots and lots of people looking. Finally, late afternoon, someone entered the old woodshed behind Miss Stewart's house and found a wet, cold, crying boy. I'm sure they had searched there lots of times during the day, but the rain and cold had finally driven him from his hiding place. Miss Stewart had asked her houseboy to make a fire.

We found out that he had hidden in the dense branches near the top of a huge cypress tree in the forest behind Miss Stewart's house. We all knew that monkeys could hide for hours in those trees, but the trees were extremely hard for us to climb. The big trees had so many branches that it was hard to squeeze between them near the top.

Billy had been in that tree most of the day and through all that rain. I don't remember much more about Billy. Maybe his parents took him out of school.

I do know that we weren't kind, sensitive, or forgiving. I think we just forgot about him when he was gone.

A Bible story about being kind is in Ruth 1:14-19

Dumb African Mud Frogs

African mud frogs are pretty dumb when they are hungry. They are so stupid you can catch them with almost anything as bait, if they are hungry and awake. We didn't have much else to fish for, and frog legs were good to eat. We looked forward to Saturdays when we would get permission to go to the dam.

Frogs lived in the black water backed up behind the old dam. The dam was at the narrow neck of the valley so that the dorm cows would have a place to drink. It wasn't much of a pond. The water from a number of small springs followed the overgrown drainage ditches and trickled into the pond from under the marsh grass in the valley. The rotten marsh grass turned the water a dark brown, like strong tea. Since the soil was really black, the water looked black. Sometimes the water became a milky color from the white clay that was used to make the dam because the cows had just been there to drink and had stirred up the bottom of the pond.

The frogs lived down in the mud and didn't have to come up for air very often. I think they hid in the bottom of the deep footprints that the cows made in the clay when they waded in to drink. The frogs had slimy smooth skin that on top was exactly the color of the mud on the bottom of the pond. They were a pale speckled grayish color on the underside. Our teacher said they got air from the water through their skin, but I wasn't so sure about that. The head was the pointed end opposite the legs. They had no neck that you could see. Their little black eyes bumped out on top when they were open but disappeared into the slimy skin when they were closed. They weren't very big frogs; a big one might be two inches long, not counting his legs, but it was the legs we wanted to cook.

When we cut the legs off at the line that looked like a row of tiny brown stitches, our hands became slimy with some whitish junk. The skin peeled off the legs easily, uncovering the white meat. We needed to catch more than 20 frogs to get enough for each guy to even get a taste. We cooked them in a tin can with Blue Band (margarine) and salt. The meat shrunk even smaller as they cooked and slipped away from the bones, but they sure smelled good. The bones were about the size of toothpicks and as white as the meat, so it was pretty hard not to eat the bones with the meat. Getting frog legs to eat was a great way to spend Saturday.

We hoped Saturday would be a hot day so the frogs would come to the top of the water to enjoy the warmth and float on the surface of the water with just their eyes showing. We could usually see the darker shape of the frog just beneath the surface. If the cows had been there and stirred up the water, there might even be lots of frogs that got mashed out of the mud and hadn't yet found a new footprint to hide in.

Even though we had no fishing poles, no line, and no lures, we still planned to catch frogs.

After we found a biggie who agreed to take us to the Kwandruma Dukas, we knew we would be able to buy some strong black thread to use for fishing line. Our parents had sent spending money, which the dorm parents kept in our envelopes. We went to ask for some and for permission to go to the Dukas. We were delighted when they said yes and got out the envelopes, writing down on the outside just how much they gave us and what was left.

We thought earthworms would be the best bait. The orange worms we found in the mud near the cow water trough behind the barn were as thin as thread. They were too small. Maybe they weren't earthworms anyway. We decided to look for grasshoppers on the way down the hill to the dam. The frogs seemed to like best the small green or brown ones that could fly, but they were the hardest to catch. The colorful grasshoppers were the easiest to catch, but they smelled bad and spit brown juice on your hand when you caught them.

There was a Black Wattle forest partway down the steep hill on the way to the dam. It was a good place to find a pole. Each of us planned to cut down a slender sapling with his pocketknife on our trip.

We didn't have any hooks. The grasshoppers just slipped off the bent pins when we tried those before and, besides, it was hard to tie the thread to the pin. Though we could tie the thread to safety pins, they weren't much better for holding the grasshopper bait.

On our way down the hill after dinner, we caught some grasshoppers and found our poles, just as we had planned. Peter ran ahead, then came rushing back to where we were still trimming the branches off our poles with our pocketknives.

"Hey you guys, come see! There is a guy lying on the grass down there with nothing on! His clothes are all spread out on top of the bushes drying in the sun." He laughed, "I guess he is drying in the sun too!"

Of course we rushed down. We would trim our poles down at the dam.

When we got there, a man was rapidly climbing up the hill on the other side. His light blue pants were still dark blue at the waist. I guess they hadn't quite gotten dry. We had almost caught a man washing and drying the only cloths he had. He probably had had a bath in the pond too; tomorrow was Sunday.

With all our noise, there weren't any frogs on the surface of the water that we could see. Maybe it was because of the guy who took his bath. We found a tiny piece of yellow Sunlight soap. I had seen the guys at the market saw Sunlight bars of soap into small pieces with a piece of nylon string. I think this piece of soap started as a fourth of a bar. Dressing so quickly, he must have forgotten it where he left it drying on the old wooden tub. He must be quite poor to have only that many cloths and such a small piece of soap. I found a big leaf and put the soap on it, off to one side, where he could find it if he came back.

We trimmed our poles and tied thread to the poles and around the middle of the grasshoppers. We were ready. Now all we had to do was wait in the sun on the soft Kikuyu grass on top of the dam. Pretty soon the frogs should come up again to bask in the warm sun.

When a frog surfaced, we would plop a grasshopper almost on top of him. He might try to swallow it whole, immediately. If a frog did, all you had to do was lift him out of

DUMB MUD FROG

the water. Some of the frogs weren't quite so dumb and would let it go and fall back into the water, but most of them we could just grab as they hung from the thread before they let go.

The frogs tried to push out of our hand when we grabbed them. They brought their back feet all the way to their head and pushed as hard as they could to slip out of our hands. If they got free, they would jump in a series of crooked hops, trying to scramble back to the safety of the muddy water. But we could easily catch them again when they came up for air. Even those that got away would take the bait again. They never learn.

After butchering one frog, we had plenty of material to use as bait. They weren't smart. They just ate because they were hungry not knowing that there was a string tied to the bait. They didn't even learn when the frog beside them was caught, not even if part of that frog was the bait the next time. They didn't even learn when they were caught once, but got away. They were really dumb!

Is it possible that we might be a little like those frogs? If it is something we want, do we just grab it even if there is a string tied to it? Are we too dumb to let go even when we find there is a string pulling us out of our safe environment and away from God? Even when a friend we know well is pulled away, can't we learn? What if he becomes the bait? If we got caught once, aren't we smart enough to run away? Running away is a good idea like the Bible says, "So flee youthful passions and pursue righteousness, faith, love, and peace, along with those who call on the Lord from a pure heart."

There are lots of things other kids want us to do with them, things we know God doesn't want us to do, something like the bait offered to the dumb African Mud Frogs. They were safe in the water until they swallowed the bait and wouldn't let go.

If we stay close to God He'll help us know the right way to go. We need to get out of any situations that can trap us into doing wrong.

The Bible story about refusing is in - Daniel 3:8-18

I Broke My Arm

I once climbed a pole to improve my view. You see, it was a little hard to see the volleyball game the Biggies were playing, especially since I was only in fourth grade.

I remember one of the biggie girls, Patsy Deans, seemed especially beautiful to me, and I thought I would be able to see her so much better from the top of the pole, the pole that held up the volleyball net. She was playing on David Brill's team and no doubt noticed him much more than the round cheeked little boy climbing up the pole. She had a nice smile and wore pretty dresses.

The principal, Mr. Miller, who was also our science teacher, had excused us all from classes in the middle of the day so we could watch the eclipse of the sun.

He had had us take small pieces of glass and get them all sooty black on one side by holding them over a burning candle. We had to hold the broken piece of glass very close to the candle to make the flame smoke.

"You need to move the glass around and around so it won't get too hot in one place, or it will break. That's because the glass will expand too much in one place and crack between there and where it is cooler. You can hold it on a corner," he explained, "because glass doesn't conduct heat very well. Move the glass and watch the coating of smoke. Try to make it an even color."

SMOKED VIEWING GLASS

He told us that if we held the piece of smoky glass up towards the sun and looked at the sun through the glass, the sun wouldn't hurt our eyes.

You know, he was right! The sun didn't look like a bright spot that made you see greenish white lines when you looked away, but it looked like a tiny orange slice of moon. Mr. Miller said the orange was the part of the sun we could see and the real moon was between the sun and us, so that part looked black. Even though we couldn't see the moon, it was there. We couldn't see it because the light from the sun was too bright. Besides, the shadow side of the moon was facing us.

Mr. Miller also told us, "When there is an eclipse of the moon, it happens at night during full moon. The earth gets in the way of the sunlight hitting the moon. The moon gets dark little by little just like the sun is getting dark now."

We kept checking the sun through our smoked pieces of glass, hoping to see the black part get bigger and the orange part get smaller, until the orange part got bigger again and the sun looked like a round spot. That all would take time, so we got out of classes. The Biggies played volleyball.

I tried the glass a few times, but the eclipse didn't change very quickly. When I put the piece of glass in my pocket, the soot got partly rubbed off, so I couldn't look at the sun any more. I could see the little white moon shaped spots of light where the sun shown down through the trees. Mr. Miller said the light spots were that shape because of the eclipse of the sun. The sunlight came through small spaces between the dark leaves of the avocado tree and those holes acted like the pinhole camera we had made in class. He was a good science teacher.

It was getting a little darker and colder right in the middle of the morning. I wondered if the chickens at the dorm would go to bed, or if it wasn't dark enough yet. I wondered how soon it would be time for lunch hoping they wouldn't have that corned beef and fried potatoes stuff again. We had that quite often. I quit looking at the crescent shaped white moons dancing around in the shadows under the tree. I knew it was the breeze that sometimes made the little white moons in the shade appear and disappear since the leaves covered up the holes in the shade. I decided to watch volleyball.

I couldn't see very well because other bigger kids were in front of me, near the sideline for volleyball, waiting to play. When somebody missed the ball or something, they got a point or somebody got to go in to play from those standing along the sideline. They called it rotating in. I decided to climb the pole. It wasn't too hard to climb now since I didn't have my cast in the way anymore. I would be able to see over those big kids if I got to the top of the pole that held up the net; I would have the perfect view.

I could see Patsy. She was just beautiful. She had on a frilly white blouse and long blue skirt with lots of extra white stuff at the bottom that got big when she twirled around. She was talking and laughing at David. When she missed the ball, he just smiled. He didn't say a lot, except when someone else missed the ball.

"Aren't you the boy with the broken arm?" It was Mr. Miller's big voice. "Get down from that pole at once!" he ordered. "And where is your cast? Didn't you break your arm just a couple of weeks ago?"

He was right; I was the boy who had broken his arm. It broke during one recess when I was racing Peter Epp from the top of the monkey bars to get a broken thermometer he'd spotted in the grass below us. They have mercury inside which makes nice tiny silver balls when it rolls around in your hand. I didn't land just right when I dropped from the bars. Peter ran off with the thermometer and never looked back to see why it took me so long to get back up.

When I swung down between the bars, I had held onto the bar too long and swung out almost level before I let go. I landed on my back with my arm underneath me. I had to roll over onto my stomach to get my knees under me. I could push with only my one hand, but I was able to get up. I couldn't brush the red dirt off my pants with both hands, but I got most of it off, at least where I could see it in front. The bell was ringing. Recess had ended.

OUR MONKEY WALK

I didn't want anyone to see my tears, and I rubbed my eyes, first on one sleeve, then on the other. In the classroom washbasin it was hard to get the red dirt off my right hand. I couldn't rub the soap between my hands. It hurt when I tried wiping my hand off on the towel. Mrs. Miller didn't like us to get dirt on our Arithmetic papers. I hung up the towel and hid the dirty part inside. I guess I got some more dirt off, but my wrist was still red and there was some dirt in a cut, but it wasn't too bad. I got to my desk on time.

Mrs. Miller came back from the staff prayer meeting, and we started Arithmetic just as Abrahamu was clanging the second bell. It hurt to hold down my paper with my right hand, and I couldn't hold my pencil very well with my other hand. When I moved my paper, I saw that it was dirty. When something wet got on my paper, I tried to wipe it off, but it smeared. My name, the date, the word Arithmetic and the page number at the top right corner of my paper were very hard to read. Mrs. Miller, my fourth grade teacher, always walked around to see if any of us needed any help. I bent very low over my work. I knew it was not neat, and it took a long time to write what I wanted. My left hand made 4's and 5's backwards and sometimes the 7's and 2's, too. The 1's were the only easy numbers. Erasing made a mess because the eraser got wet somehow.

I smelled Mrs. Miller's perfume. She was very close to my desk, maybe looking over my shoulder. I was ashamed of my messy paper because I liked to make it just like she taught us. I didn't want her to see. Her shiny black shoes and the hem of her long dress came into my view. She was looking at the messy title of my paper; I was sure. Maybe she knew I was silently crying. Gently she asked me, "Paul Henry, is something wrong?"

I couldn't hold it in any more. I just blurted out in a loud sobbing voice, "I broke my arm."

It turned out that it was broken. Miss Wentworth said so. She was the nurse at the hospital. She was very gentle and moved my fingers and turned my wrist a little one way, then the other. Each time she asked if it hurt. I had to say yes over and over. They got on the radio and decided to take me to my Dad to fix my arm.

Mr. Schuit took my big sister and me a long ways away to Aba where my dad could check my arm. Mom and Dad were at Aba because my little brother Timmy had died; that's where they had buried him. Dad said he died from Malaria. My dad was a doctor.

I don't remember much about Timmy. I only saw him during vacation time. I do remember him and Winnie hanging over the back seat of our old Plymouth and singing, "I've worked for the Lord for a long, long time, and I ain't got weary yet." We got tired of that song. Then they chanted, "There is a truck ahead of us. There is a truck ahead of us. There is a truck ahead of us," over and over again, until finally we met one. Then they started to chant, "There is a truck behind us; there is a truck behind us," until Dad said to stop. Then we played Bridge. The first one to see a bridge would yell out, "BRIDGE!" If it turned out to be a shadow, you got points off. It was a long trip to Aba, but there were 27 bridges. I think Mom and my younger sister, Winnie, missed Timmy the most.

We finally got there, and my dad checked my arm in the fluoroscope and showed me the lighter line on one of my pale green arm bones that showed up on the screen. His ring made almost a white circle around the bone of his finger. It seemed to float in space around his finger bone. His bones looked whiter than mine on the screen. My skin hardly even made a shadow in the glowing green. Dad said it was cracked, but that it was in good alignment. He put on a cast. I couldn't even straighten my elbow, or move my wrist.

Mr. Schuit brought us back to Rethy, and Mom and Dad went back to their hospital at Banda.

That was a long time before the eclipse of the sun. The cast had gotten wet, and just today I had used my pocket knife to unwind all the gauze and cut the soggy plaster off. I had dropped it down the outhouse hole when I got permission to go to the TO during school. My arm looked white and skinny when it came off. Now Mr. Miller was looking at my skinny arm and was probably comparing it with the other plump tanned one.

"You get down to the hospital right now, and get Miss Wentworth to look at your arm," he said.

She was a smart nurse. She cleaned my skinny white arm and wrapped it in soft wide gauze. She added some white surgical tape, lots wider than what my mom used to seal my peanut butter tin. I didn't know they made it that wide. She didn't make it very tight. She told me to be careful. Mr. Miller saw the clean wrappings and knew the nurse had done a good job, so he was pleased. I was happy too. It wasn't heavy and soggy any more, and it didn't even stink.

It wasn't long before the gauze under the tape got all wet and the tape got dirty too. The tape was still pretty sticky when I tried to unwind it. The scissors from school didn't cut it too well, but my arm felt good when I finally got it all off and dropped the scraps down the deep TO hole.

My arm healed just fine.

Sometimes we are sure we know best. We try to hide our problems like that little boy with a broken arm. I really needed help, though, didn't I? We are trying so hard when Jesus wants to help us. He said, "Come to me, all who labor and are heavy laden, and I will give you rest. Take my yoke upon you, and learn from me, for I am gentle and lowly in heart, and you will find rest for your souls."

I thought I could hide my broken arm, but I couldn't. God had just the right people there to help me, even though I didn't want their help. Sometimes we need to admit that we can't do everything all by ourselves, even though we try.

The Bible story is in Luke 8:43–48

Without Any Real Friends

I can still remember what I felt like one time when Lester asked me, "Who said you could come along?" A little fifth grade boy away from home at a boarding school has to have friends. There was no mom or dad there to run to. They were 550 miles away at a mission station doing surgery in the hospital and telling people about Jesus. There was no telephone. The short wave radio was for important things, not for kids talking to their parents. No one would tattle to the dorm parents. It just wasn't done; it was against the kids' code.

Letters went out only if some missionary was traveling in the direction the letters needed to go. The letters would be dropped off somewhere along the way to be picked up by the next traveling missionary until they eventually got to the destination on the envelope. We wrote letters to our moms and dads every week as part of our writing class in school. The teacher read them and sealed them. Mine went in the box for Zandeland. The stack might eventually get there at mid term, six weeks after the first letter was written for the teacher.

Having friends was the most important thing, but you didn't know that until you had none. Little boys thought hunting birds was one of the most important things. Lester told the best hunting stories and knew the names of all the birds. He could make lots of bird sounds, just like the birds, and he knew which bird made which sounds. He could find the birds' nests and could tell by the color of the shell and its pattern what kind of bird laid the eggs. The way the nest was woven showed him what kind of bird had made it. Everybody wanted to be his friend.

That Saturday morning before breakfast, Lester and Gary were sharpening their arrows. They had been shooting at trees, at leaves on the ground, and in the air all Friday evening and had dulled their best arrows. Abrahamu made us arrows from a tall weed he knew and put chicken feathers through a small slit in one end to make them fly straight. About one third of the arrows would whirl or wobble, but some flew very straight and true. They each needed to be tested in order to get the best ones for hunting. Sliding the feather back a little or trimming it slightly sometimes helped. When we got the arrows, they were really sharp, but after testing, they needed sharpening again.

I was sitting on the ground near Lester and Gary while they sharpened their arrows, happy to be included. I was fixing my homemade slingshot. One of the main red rubber strips, which had been cut with a razor from an old bicycle inner tube, had broken again. I was shortening the other one and retying both with the slender rubber strips to the crotch of the branch. Hunting with my slingshot was my plan. We were headed out to the dorm forest, a small Black Wattle woods behind the school. Lester was first, of course, Gary next, and I last. They had their bows and arrows. I had my slingshot. My pockets were bulging with carefully selected rocks. It was great. I thought Lester was the best hunter. I was going to have the best Saturday!

Maybe we would get a Yellow Bum. We often saw those fruit-eaters with the black head and the yellow feathers under their tail. Yellow Bums usually hid somewhere on the wild blackberry bushes near the forest. If we got one, we'd make a little campfire in the woods and roast the tiny bird on a stick.

The roasted bird would get shared. Maybe I would get a leg. Lester would get the breast meat of course. I could at least have the back and wings after they took off the breast meat and legs. I hoped they wouldn't roast it so long that the wings were burned black. To have friends to hunt with on Saturday was the best thing I could think of.

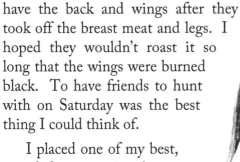

SLING SHOT.

I placed one of my best, rounded stones in the small leather pouch of my slingshot. I saved my chipped marble to shoot in case we saw one of the small black and white hornbills that were sometimes in the forest. They have big, red and yellow beaks. I held the loquat tree crotch in my left hand, my thumb and first finger on each side of the "Y". I stretched the rubber experimentally. It felt just right, neither side of the rubber was stronger. It pulled evenly. I wanted to be ready. We were crossing the cow pasture, about to enter the forest. I was mimicking Lester's footsteps, very careful not to make any noise. Gary's lug grip shoes weren't as quiet as my Kedd sneakers. He stepped right on the stick Lester had so carefully stepped over. Since we might see a bird, I was trying to be perfectly quiet. It was then that Lester stopped and turned to ask me, "Who said you could come along?"

I had no answer. I stopped. Silently, I turned around and followed our trail back through the dew soaked grass, plodding back towards the dorm. The little stone tumbled to the ground from the limp pouch of my slingshot. I was rejected, all alone. They didn't want me. I emptied the rocks from my pockets.

Maybe my big sister was somewhere around. At breakfast, Mr. Schuit had told me that I had a package from home, which he had given to my sister. I had forgotten all about that. Maybe I could go get my part and not have my roommates see me open it. They usually knew when I got a package from home since Mr. Schuit passed out the mail in the dining hall. This time he had given it to her, and they had not seen it. They were off hunting.

Mom always used a cardboard box from medicines shipped in for my dad's hospital. She put stuff in it for my sister and me. Since my sister was older, she got to divide it up. I didn't need to worry about the girls or the Titchies, but the Biggie boys and my roommates could finish off everything if they came in when I opened my package. Now would be a good time, on Saturday, in the middle of the morning when the dorm was nearly empty.

It was almost like a miracle! My sister was on the low wall beside the steps in front of their dorm playing with the biggie girls' cat. Actually it was the Schuits' cat, but the girls always had it and played with it. They even put perfume on it; at least that's what the guys said. She heard me call her from the brick walk boundary between the girls' and boys' side and somehow knew exactly what I wanted. Without even coming to talk to me, she just went into her dorm and came out with the opened box. "Here is your share," she said and dropped it in front of me.

The cat was just settling down after walking around in a circle where they had been sitting on the wall in the sunshine. That was probably the warmest spot. My sister returned to her side of the lawn, picked up the cat, and sat down on the low wall again. I wished I had a pet.

The package had the usual goodies in it: the dried boos were wrapped in wax paper; the roasted flying ants were in an orange Bourneville tin; Mom's good cookies were in a Klim tin. There was also an oatmeal tin of fresh, Zande, peanut butter, the lid taped on with surgical tape.

The Zande women make the best peanut butter there is. They grind it three times between smooth stones. The Zandes grow the peanuts, dig them up, and dry them in the sun before they are opened to harvest the nuts. They roast the peanuts over an open fire on a pan made from a drum top, stirring them all the time so none burn. They take off all the red skins and break the nuts in half to take out all the tiny bitter peanut germs. We called those pieces the Santa because they looked a little like a man with a beard. When they pour the nuts in the wind, the tiny stuff blows away. After pounding the peanuts in a Sangu, they grind them between the stones. The bottom stone is big and flat, and the grinding stone is about the size of a big cob of corn. The women kneel behind the big smooth stone and roll and rub the crushed nuts between the stones until they are creamy and smooth. Zande peanut butter is the best!

The big yellow and brown Klim tin held the peanut butter cookies where it used to have dried milk powder. Klim is milk spelled backwards. I liked to eat the milk powder by licking it off my wet finger. Since it stuck to the roof of my mouth, I tasted it for a long time. I liked Klim better than the other kinds of instant milk. The cookies weren't even a little stale. Mom probably baked them just before Mr. Dix came down for the mid-term Field Council meetings that were going on. Not even half were broken. My sister was fair. She probably took some of the broken ones in her half. I got half, even though I was smaller.

I snuck back to my room and hid the box under my bed. I didn't have a bunk bed anymore, and the bedspread hung nearly to the floor, so it was the best place I had to hide my stuff from Mom. I found a book and took out a cookie. I kept the tin of cookies handy, just under the bedspread where I could easily reach another one and settled down to read.

It was quiet. Maybe it wasn't so bad to be alone. Zane Grey talked about girls in his book but mostly about frontiersmen and Indians. Jonathan liked Betty Zane, but he would never tell her. He protected all the settlers and was almost as great a woodsman as Wetzel. Wetzel grew his black hair down to his shoulders. He taunted the Indians who wanted his scalp and called him Deathwind.

Unexpectedly, the door burst open with a bang. In sauntered Peter and Kenny, my other two roommates. "Hey that smells good; any cookies this time?" Peter asked. Then they asked again, almost at the same time, "What else did you get? Aren't you gonna share?

"I got some dried boos and some flying ants," I said.

"We don't want that stuff. Didn't you get anything else?" they persisted.

"I got some peanut butter too, but no chocolate chip cookies like last time," I was trying to get them to go away and do something else, besides, the cookies were a different kind.

They were looking for something in their drawers. I went back to reading, lying on my bed. They looked like they were almost ready to go out again, but Bruce Weise came in. "Hey, gimmie a couple of those cookies," he said. "They are really good. Your sister gave me one."

I think my sister liked Bruce, but I think she liked his big brother David more. She probably gave him a cookie so David would hear about them and maybe hint that he would like one as well. Maybe she would have wasted five on David.

Bruce was a biggie. He could easily beat me up. I reached under my bed and dragged out the Klim tin of cookies.

"Hey, did your sister only give you the broken ones?" Bruce asked as he helped himself to several. Peter and Kenny came over.

"I thought I smelled cookies," Peter said. "How come you hid them?" He took a handful. Kenny took some quickly, before Bruce took some more. I took a couple.

"Boy, these are really good!" they said. "Do ya have any more?"

"That is all the cookies I have," I said. They took some more.

"Thanks for sharing. You're a great guy," they said. "Be seeing you around." They slammed the door as they left.

I poured the last of the crumbs into my hand and slid the empty Klim tin under my bed. I put the book open, upside down, under my pillow and smoothed my bed. Maybe I could find a chameleon in the Lantana hedge in front of the Titchie Dorm. I could play with him. He might like to sit on my finger.

What is it like to be unpopular, to have no friends? What if the one you thought was including you asked you to leave?

Jesus can be your best friend, yet He was hated more than any man. He called us friends. "It is the LORD your God who goes with you. He will not leave you or forsake you." He is a friend that sticks closer than a brother.

The Bible story is in 1 Samuel 20:14-23; 2 Samuel 9:2-3

To Tell the Truth

When I was at Rethy, I told a story about my Silver Pocket Ben, my most prized possession. It was very expensive, made of sterling silver and studded with jewels. On the back was an engraving done by a master engraver in Antwerp who used a diamond tipped stylus. The "*PHB*" was in Edwardian Script. It kept nearly perfect time, loosing less than 15 seconds in a week. My dad gave it to me. It was originally owned by his great-great grandfather, an engineer on the Chesapeake and Ohio passenger train. His name had the same initials as my and my dad's name. It had to be an accurate watch because the train was required to be on time to the minute. Unfortunately, it doesn't keep quite as well now as it did then.

Well, it wasn't really solid silver, but it was shinny, with a chrome-plated bezel and a chrome-plated copper back. I guess it wasn't really studded with jewels either. In fact, well, there were none. It didn't really keep nearly perfect time, but it did work once. Although, at the time I told that story, it didn't work at all. It was the first pocket watch I ever had, and my dad did give it to me, so that made it my most prized possession. That part of the story was true. It was actually the cheapest "Pocket Ben" watch that Westclox made. I don't even know the name of my great-great-great grandfather. Maybe he was an engineer on a train, but I have no idea. I was just lying.

Have you ever wished you were popular? Have you wished that others listened to you eagerly, that they wanted you with them? Maybe you wished that they wanted you to be their best friend, or you even wished that the girls thought you were handsome and smart. Have you ever dreamed that they wanted you to sit by them? When I told the guys about my watch, I wanted the other boys to like me. (I wasn't interested in girls quite yet.) I really, truly wanted a friend, cross my heart and hope to die. I told the story to make them like me, but the story wasn't true.

My stories weren't as exciting as the other boys' stories. I had never shot an elephant with a .375, nor had I wrestled with a twenty-foot python. I hadn't hunted buffalos that vacation. In fact, my dad rarely went hunting. He didn't even have a .375. His gun was an octagonal barreled lever action 32/40 with an eight bullet tubular magazine below the barrel and one more in the chamber. His shotgun was a 1929 Hercules made by Montgomery Ward. I only had a .177 pellet gun.

Billy Faulkner gave the pellet gun to me. Actually, he threw it down after he broke the stock. He was disgusted because it was so weak. I asked if I could have it. With the help of the Zande carpenter who worked for us, I made a new Mahogany stock for his old gun. I pushed every pellet through the barrel of that gun with a long palm straw from our Zande-made broom. That wore the lead pellets down against the rifling so they wouldn't get stuck in the barrel. I oiled each pellet too, and I did get some birds. I really did. That's the truth, but what is that against shooting an elephant with a mighty .375, or was it a .400 caliber elephant gun? I never got a Crested Hawk Eagle with my pellet gun. My stories just weren't very interesting. Never would I tell them the time I tried to hit a Wagtail on top of the roof of Miss Schauer's house and hit the hedge in front of the house instead. My pellet gun wasn't very powerful. At least the pellet missed the front window of her house and didn't get stuck in the barrel like sometimes happened.

I told you about the time the other boys let me come hunting with them, at least I had assumed they did. I thought I was finally included, a boy that fit in, a boy with friends. But, I remember to this day the sinking feeling I had when they turned, just as they entered the forest, and said, "Who said you could come?" Without an answer I was dejected and turned back to the dorm, once again alone.

My pet crow, however, liked me. He would hear me mimic his "caw," and knew it was me coming home from school. He would "caw" back, and I'd go find him. I always went to see how he was doing in the little cage he stayed in during school. Since following me to school one time, he had to stay there until I came home. He would be sitting in his cage fluttering his wings in and out at his sides, just waiting for me. He wasn't trying to fly, just shaking his wings the way he did when he was hungry. He always seemed to be hungry. I let him out and headed for the dorm kitchen. Sometimes I could get food scraps to feed him.

He even liked cold mashed potatoes. He would sit there shaking his wings, cawing, but keeping his beak open and pointed straight up. It was all pink inside, and I could see his little triangular tongue. I would drop in a glob of mashed potatoes, and he would stretch up and jerk his head back and forth trying to eat the whole glob at once. He didn't have all his adult feathers yet and the edges of his beak were still soft and pink at the back. I had gotten him when he was maybe a week old.

I wasn't the only one who had a crow. The little African boy had brought three in the old Blue Band cardboard box he probably got from some missionary. Most likely he had climbed a Eucalyptus tree to a crow's big, old, messy nest and just thrown the little crows down.

The African boys watch the nests. When just one crow is flying around, instead of two, the eggs are being incubated. Later, when two are flying back and forth, they are feeding the baby crows. They know how long to wait before climbing those big trees so the little crows have enough wing feathers to slow their fall; otherwise the kids at the dorm wouldn't buy the baby crows. I got last pick, but I liked my little crow, and he seemed to like me. Gary's crow was getting glossy black feathers first, and it could almost fly. He sometimes carried it on his shoulder. I didn't have the best looking crow. He didn't have such nice feathers, was a messy eater, and didn't preen very much, but he was my friend.

I did have that watch, and one day the boys were talking about watches. I was listening, and I knew they were exaggerating their stories because I had taken my watch apart and put it back together, well sort of. I knew something about watches, a lot they didn't know.

BALANCE ASSEMBLY SHOWING INCABLOCK JEWELING

There was a hairspring attached to the balance wheel axle and to the top plate of the watch to make the balance wheel swing back to the center in exactly the right amount of time. In my "Pocket Ben," that spring was now loose and bent beyond repair. I had tried to straighten it, but the tweezers that weren't good enough for my Dad to use in eye

47 -

surgery any more weren't good enough for watch repair either. The tiny pin that slides into the hole in the post on the top plate to hold the end of the hairspring in place had popped out of the tweezers when I tried to put it back, and I couldn't find it. It was smaller than one millimeter cut off the point of a very sharp, thin needle. It was made of copper, so I couldn't find it with a magnet either.

There was also a mainspring, which was very hard to get back in once I pulled it out. As it unwound, it made the watch go. A wheel with saw-shaped teeth pushed the pin lever to the side each time it hit a little shiny pin on the under side of the balance wheel. The balance spring brought the wheel back again, keeping it swinging back and forth to count the seconds. The wheel with the saw-shaped teeth moved one tooth at a time, letting the mainspring slowly unwind, rotating the hands around the face at the right speed. There were gears to make the little hand just go a little way every time the big hand went all the way around. My Westclox Pocket Ben was now certainly beyond repair, but I knew something they didn't know about watches, and I started my story.

It was true at first, but they were listening to me, really listening, and I needed a longer, better story, so my watch became better than the cheap Westclox Pocket Ben my dad gave me. My skills at watch repair mounted by the minute as I related all I had done to the watch. When I told about the hairspring, they were really interested, but I ran out of story. It started out true, but I didn't really fix my watch after it had dropped from my bunk bed. I hadn't landed on it when I jumped down to get it, and I hadn't made a new hairspring. It didn't work mostly because I took it all apart and couldn't get it back together without spoiling it. I actually did get it back together and only lost one tiny screw besides the balance spring hold pin. It didn't keep perfect time. In fact it didn't keep time at all.

Then Andy said, "I don't believe you."

You know, he was right, and I had nothing to say. I knew God didn't want me to lie. Why didn't I just tell the truth? I felt terrible and more alone than ever when the boys laughed at me. Now God wasn't happy with me either. I went off to stand by myself, at the edge of our playing field where it sloped down to the second level, but they followed me. Beneath my favorite blue shorts my chunky legs somehow caught Andy Englebrect's attention, and he laughed, "Look at his double jointed knees!" He poked at the back of my knees. They did bump forward and back, so they must have been double jointed just like he said.

Why do we lie? It seems it is usually for selfish reasons; to look better, to impress someone, to get something or to get out of something.

Have you ever thought that your lie really hurts you more than anyone else? What you say in the future is now less likely to be truthful, isn't it? Isn't your conscience that part of you that is, or should be, sensitive to God? He said, "You shall not steal; you shall not deal falsely; you shall not lie to one another. You shall not swear by my name falsely, and so profane the name of your God: I am the LORD."

The young boy I told you about grew up and learned a whole lot more about watches, but especially he remembers the long-term futility of lying. He also never wore shorts again, though the main problem with his legs now is that they are getting old.

Love each other and tell the truth.

The Bible reading is in Ephesians 4:15-25

Why Was That so Bad

This is stupid. Why should I have to sit here? What is so bad about waking up a little early anyway? It is Saturday. I wasn't the only one talking.

Remember the old dam where I used to catch mud frogs, the dam that was made so the cows would have a place to drink in the valley at Rethy? Sometimes the mud frogs wouldn't take our grasshopper bait, or they would just stay down in the mud if it was cold. On those kinds of days we ended up wading in the shallow water. We tried to keep our pants dry, or we might be asked why they were wet when we got back to the dorm.

There wasn't really enough water to swim in, but it was the closest to a swimming hole that we ever had. The bottom of the pond, where the mud frogs used to hide near the dam, was slimy gray clay. The clay would gush up between our toes, and we would sink in until the water was nearly to our knees. If we rolled our pants up extra high, they might only get partly wet. Once our legs dried, they were white and flaky from the clay. Further out, where it was deeper, it was black mud and rotting marsh grass. We had to feel ahead with our feet so that we wouldn't suddenly step in an old drainage ditch made when there were gardens in that part of the valley. The dorm parents might get mad if we came back sopping wet. Besides, it got cold if you got too wet. We used to go there every Saturday if we got permission to go out of bounds. Sometimes, we were even allowed to swim if the Dorm parent was with us.

Saturdays were the best days, and here I was sitting all by myself on the island of grass by the flowerbed. It wasn't really an island, just a circle of grass with a rose garden in the center. It was like an island since the red dirt road went all the way around it. It was where cars could turn around when they came to the place between the dorms. Right now it was my prison. I was being punished.

PADDLE
WHEEL

I sat there thinking about all the neat things I could be doing. I even had my pocket-knife, an Okapi knife with shiny red, blue and yellow colored plastic on the handle. It was in my pocket. I had gotten it for five franks at a duka in Kwandruma. Just last week, I had made a little paddle-wheel at the dam with it.

The water had been too cold to wade very much, but the sun was warm so we were playing by the old wooden bathtub. The tub had been made by hollowing out some big old log long ago, but it had rotted and now wasn't even good enough for a boat anymore. Some of the big boys had tried to use it like a boat, but it was so waterlogged and leaky that in the end they gave up. Now it was half sunk, upside down in the mud, and the Africans used it as a place to pound their clothes when they washed them at the dam. You could tell because the soap made the exposed wood white when it dried. They liked to wash their clothes there because it was easier than carrying the water up the hill to their hut. Their clothes could also be dried on the marsh reeds out in the hot sunshine on a good day.

Last week, though, the water trickled slowly past the tub and was nearly clear since the cows hadn't been there recently to drink. That's where I had made my paddle-wheel. The trickle of water went down the face of the dam before it disappeared into the marsh.

Just sitting there in my grass and rose-garden island prison, on a Saturday, was pretty boring. I wondered if my little paddlewheel was still working from last week. Probably, the paddles made from sections of wide marsh grass blades had withered, turned brown, and twisted. It wouldn't work if that had happened. Maybe a little African boy had smashed it, or maybe he had fixed it. The reed I had used for the axle wasn't nearly as good as the axle I had just whittled from the dead rose bush stem while sitting here. Since I had used the trickle of water near where the Africans washed their clothes, they probably spoiled the little sluiceway. I had built it on reed stilts to bring the water over my little wheel. It was hard to get it going properly, but it was flipping nicely with a little plop, plop, plop sound when I left last Saturday. Probably a cow stepped on it.

Why did Mr. Schuit have to spoil my Saturday anyway? It wasn't fair. All the other guys got to go down to the dam, and some of them were talking this morning too. I heard they might even get to swim. I had put my blue shorts on under my khaki pants just in case we could swim, but Mr. Schuit had seen me as we went by the rose garden and something made him say,

"You were talking this morning before six, weren't you?"

It was true, so what could I say? I didn't look at him, but I mumbled, "Yes."

"You've been told not to talk before the first bell before, haven't you?" he said. He looked very big and a little scary, and I couldn't really look up at him.

That was true too. I hung my head even further and mumbled, "Uh huh."

We had all been on the way to the dam. Some of the guys were running ahead. Now I was just standing there looking at my old black and white high top Keds, my favorite sneakers even though there was a hole in the front of the right one. They were too small, I guess, but the very best for running down the hill to the dam. I wiggled my right big toe a little. My toe peeked out through the hole in my socks. They were drooping down over the top on my sneakers since the elastic didn't hold them up any more. Mr. Schuit was quiet for what seemed like a long time. Maybe I was supposed to say "sorry" or something, but I just stood there. I didn't think there was anything wrong with talking a tiny bit before six on Saturday, especially since I hadn't even gotten out of bed. I said nothing. Finally he said, "Well, you can't go to the dam today. You just stay here."

Then he walked off. I sat. I sat down on the thick Kikuyu grass on the low bank inside the circle of red road by the Dorm, the rose garden behind me. I sat there for hours.

Was that fair to make me sit there all morning and not let me go to the dam and swim with the other guys just because I talked before the stupid bell?

Who decides what is fair anyway?

Once God told all the Israelites over 20 years old, except two, that they would have to die in the desert. They had to wander around for nearly forty more years and weren't allowed to go into the land God had promised to them. It seems it was just because ten of the twelve men who went in as spies came back saying they could never defeat the people in that land; was that fair? All those people decided to believe the ten spies rather than the two who said the Lord would help them win like He had promised. The story is in the Bible.

I guess in the end it is God who decides what is fair, even if we can't understand why something happens. I think I learned a good lesson that day, sitting on the grass.

I stayed there in my open prison, carving little things from rose bush sticks until the first dinner bell rang at noon. Then I left to wash my hands. The rules said we had to be to dinner on time, and we had to wash our hands.

I guessed I didn't need to sit there anymore.

The Bible story is in Numbers 14:29–38 & 26:64, 65

Ever Heard a Pied Wagtail?

Tweet tweet tweeet... tweeteet twwo youu

Tweet tweet tweeet... tweeteet twwo youu

Did you recognize it?

No...? It was supposed to be a wild bird, not a chicken.

This bird's call is actually very easy.

It is very friendly and curious.

It is called by some, "Ndege ya Mungini" (bird of the home.)

It even fights a its own reflection in your windows, if they are clean that is.

It will make a nest under the eaves of a house.

Its tan eggs are spotted light brown.

It flies for short distances in front of a car (a slow car in Congo), alights, runs, flies again, then dips down to flutter and lands again, running just after it lands.

When it lands, it dips its tail up and down a number of times.

It has a distinct black "V" on the front of its white chest.

It is all Black and White.

It is called a Pied Wagtail. Be sure to check the color of the eggs.

Years ago in Congo I used to watch the Wagtails on the cement steps just outside the door of the school while I sat stuck at my desk. The Wagtail was free to fly away; I wasn't. I had to study, so... I watched the Wagtail catching flies that landed on the warm steps in the sunshine.

Since the door was wide open, we had the option of catching flies as well. Lester was the best. If I moved my cupped hand slowly enough, I could get quite near the fly before sweeping my hand above him to make the capture. If the fly was crouched down, ready to take off, he might be too fast. But, if he was walking or polishing his wings with his prickly back legs, it would be easy.

Studying Biology was part of the school curriculum. Captured flies provided unofficial, unrecognized, and perhaps unapproved, material for experimentation. A fly with one third of each wing clipped off can still fly, but it looses altitude. Flight with one wing is not successful. The fly must get dizzy en route to the floor. A thread tied to a fly is too heavy for him to carry, but a Carpenter Bumblebee does fine on a 15-foot tether.

Rats are said to be smart enough to learn their way through a maze. Of course they get a food reward. They probably just smell the food and follow their noses. Flies aren't too smart in mazes. We weren't allowed to carve the mahogany top of our desks, but I found that the soft packing board pine, that made the bookshelf of my desk, was easily modified to make a fly-size maze of little ditches. Covered with a clear plastic ruler, the progress of the fly through the maze could be "scientifically" observed. Maybe the trauma of wing removal caused the fly's lack of interest in seeking the open exit.

Wagtails, being the friendly birds they were, became the first target of many a young hunter. I stood by, watching Danny Nelson with his smoking gun poised to shoot his first wagtail.

"Tweet tweet tweeet... tweeteet twwo youu;

Tweet tweet tweeet... tweeteet twwo youu," sang the unconcerned Wagtail sitting on the edge of the roof. The gun was smoking, not because Danny had already shot and was waiting for the projectile to reach the bird, but because the wind was causing the candle in the Nestles Condensed milk can to burn poorly. Danny was sighting along the top of the pen filler barrel of his gun, waiting for the explosion that would launch the projectile.

You see, the gun was a muzzle-loader that used the candle heat to ignite the discharge. The powder was the yellow sulfur mixture that we had scraped from the head of the red, wax coated, Union Matches that we could get for a few Franks in the Dukas. The barrel was a cleaned out copper pen filler with one end crimped over. Using a bicycle spoke for the ramrod, we poured in the sulfur powder from the match heads and then the packing (some chewed up, but not too wet, paper) ramming it all in gently with the bicycle spoke. The bullet was last, a piece of cut off nail pushed in carefully with a last bit of

SULFER UNION MATCH HEAD

PIECE OF CUT NAIL

WAD

PEN FILLER BARREL

AIR VENT

CANDLE HEAT SOURCE

SECTION CONDENSED MILK CAN

DETAIL VIEW — DANNY'S GUN

packing. A Nestles Condensed Milk can, with a candle burning inside, was just the right size to make it a real handgun.

We learned a lot at school, like Newton's Laws of Motion. The experimental models of the muzzleloader verified the one about the action and equal and opposite reaction. With the pen filler fully charged with two match heads, the wadding, the piece of nail, and a little more wadding, we balanced it on top of an oatmeal can that held the burning candle. Everything was on the floor in our dorm room. Against the bed on one side of our narrow room we had placed a Barring Biscuit cover in front of the tiny gun to see what kind of penetration we might get. We sat on another bed behind the gun, out of the danger area, and waited for action. Experimental goggles, now required for Science experiments, probably still aren't imported into Congo. We certainly didn't expect the barrel to burst, but Scientists determine these things experimentally.

BANG.... Ow, ow, ow.....OWh!... OUCH!

The barrel hadn't burst. The Barring Biscuit tin cover had a hole in it, but so did Peter's leg. That's what the "Ow, ow, ow,..." was all about. The little nail bullet went one way, at high speed I guess, and the pen filler gun went the opposite way, probably more slowly. They went in opposite directions, just like Newton said. The same force, the exploding match heads ("F" in the second law) accelerated ("a") two pieces of mass ("m") in opposite directions. F = ma. The little mass went faster; the bigger one went slower. Newton's a pretty smart guy. Now that other law, where an object in motion continues in motion in a straight line unless there is an outside force acting on it, had a leg as the outside force stopping the pen filler. The leg worked. I guess it hurt too, but it stopped the pen filler. Neat huh?

Well that experiment resulted in Peter losing interest in the project. Danny, however, saw clearly that the barrel had to be wired to the Nestlé's Condensed Milk Can. That two match heads had plenty of power was clearly verified, since the nail went through the tin, the bedspread, the blankets hanging down from the bed, and even made a dent in the pembi wall behind the bed. A Wagtail would truly be a viable target.

Back to waiting for the explosion... By now Danny's hand must have been be getting hot, but surely the gun would go off soon. He adjusted his aim as the Wagtail wagged its tail and walked further up the roof. Danny didn't seem quite so steady any more. Maybe his hand was really hot!

Tweet tweet tweeet... tweeteet twwo youu

Tweet tweet tweeet... tweeteet twwo youu

Ow, ow, ow,.. OWH!~ and some other words ended the hunt. Danny didn't look too happy licking his burnt hand. The candle was certainly out due to the violent throw Danny had given his little gun. The hunt was over.

Tweet tweet tweeet... tweeteet twwo youu

Tweet tweet tweeet... tweeteet twwo youu

So what are you learning at school?

Many of the kids from Rethy went on to finish high school at Rift Valley Academy in Kenya where they have one of the best programs for college prep anywhere in the world. RVA kids score way too high on the PSAT, SAT, AP, ACT, GCSE, ABC, and other alphabetical exercises to blame it all on their smart parents. All this is in an environment where creativity is not stifled. Well... making pen filler guns, homemade firecrackers, and mazes for flies might not be "totally approved," but they do have a great variety of programs to encourage and develop every skill.

But does all this result in becoming really wise? Can you

UNION MATCH
YELLOW MATCH HEADS
STRING
NAIL
LEAD POURED IN BAMBOO SECTION MOLD
HOMEMADE FIRECRACKER

resist the pressure from your peers to do what they want you to do? Can you live without looking cool, acting cool, being cool? Can you turn off a video that isn't worth watching, just walk away from it, or throw away a book that is really just trash? I'm not talking about Calculus books.

You know we didn't have any www dot anything. We didn't even have B quality mail. We had no computers, no videos, no phones, not even any BIC pens, but our pens had copper fillers, not just plastic.

We learned lots of things, but the most important thing was learning to know God. God hasn't changed at all. Knowing Him and loving Him is the only reason life makes any sense. The Bible says, "Trust in the LORD with all your heart, and do not lean on your own understanding. In all your ways acknowledge him, and he will make straight your paths. Be not wise in your own eyes; fear the LORD, and turn away from evil."

We thought we were pretty smart with all we could do with Union Matches, copper pen fillers, melted battery lead and other springs and things, but we weren't. The Bible is the source of true wisdom.

The Bible reading is Proverbs 3:1-18

The Morning Hunt

Saturday mornings are the best time of the week, if you have a pellet gun that is. I had one, but the dorm parents didn't know I had it. The earlier you got up and got to the cow pastures in the valley, the better the hunting. The dorm parents didn't like us to get up early for some reason I could never understand.

My parents knew I wanted a pellet gun. They saw me look longingly at the BSA in the Greek's shop every time we went through Doruma and stopped to shop on the way home from Rethy. The Greek even let me try it. He seemed happy that I was so interested. He showed me how to cock it by holding the stock between my legs and pulling down on the barrel till the gun was nearly bent in half. If I could get it to click, it would be cocked, but it was a strong spring. If my hands were sweaty, the barrel might slip before it clicked and snap straight up to hit me in the head with the front sight at the end of the barrel. Once cocked, the barrel would stay at the open angle and I could insert the pellet, rounded end first, into the little hole in the barrel. Then I would close it, and the gun was ready to shoot.

There were lots of noisy, black-headed, golden, weaverbirds, called Village Weavers, hanging and bobbing under their nests in the tree near the Greek's shop. Some just sat on a nearby branch and fluttered their wings as they chattered at each other, totally ignoring me. I held the gun and lined up the sights. I could see the middle of the little V of the near back sight, the post of the front sight at the end of the barrel, and the golden breast of the nearest bird. My heart was pounding with excitement as the gun wobbled around and around. The bird just sat there. I shot. All went suddenly quiet except for the flutter of wings as the birds flew. That bird hadn't really been in any danger.

That vacation, Billy Faulkner had his pellet gun out and I was watching him try to hit a little condensed milk can he had set up on a stick in his front yard. Kneeling on the front porch, he rested his gun on the low brick wall railing. He shot over and over. His sister laughed, but I tried to be polite. He cocked his gun so easily; I thought he must be pretty strong.

Then he suddenly got mad. He used the gun like a club and hit the low wall with the stock. It broke. "Stupid gun," he said as he threw it off the porch.

"Can I have it?" I asked as I ran down the steps and around front to rescue it from the red ironstone gravel around the thorny red cactus flower border.

"Sure, I don't care," he said. I became the new owner of an old Gakaddo .177 pellet gun with a broken stock and a weak spring. He gave me some pellets too.

I spent the rest of the vacation with that gun. First, the carpenter and I made a new stock from Mahogany. He was a

Zande hunter and a good carpenter. My Dad may have had other jobs for him, but the carpenter understood me. I found that oiling helped the spring. I put some of Dad's 3 in 1 oil down the little hole where the air blast would come out. That helped the power. I also took a long palm frond straw from our broom and pushed each pellet through the barrel to wear it down and make it slide easier when I would shoot it. I even oiled the pellets. That gun needed all the help I could give it.

I could cock that gun with ease. I became an excellent shot, but now the weakness of the gun gave the birds the advantage they needed. I took the gun apart and the two pieces fit in my suitcase when I went back to school. Mom packed the rest. I don't remember telling her or asking her if I could take it with me. I now had a gun at Rethy and could hardly wait for Saturday morning to come!

I went to bed on Friday with my clothes on. If I lay very carefully under the spread, on top of my covers, I wouldn't need to make my bed in the morning. I could get down in my stocking feet from my top bunk and put my shoes on in the hallway, and no one would wake up.

When I woke up, it was still quite dark. It didn't matter that I had no idea what time it was. I could just barely see. I slid my gun from under the covers beside me and carefully climbed down the end of the bed nearest the door. The bed creaked a little, but my roommates never stirred. I tried to straighten the spread on my bed and then picked up my gun and my shoes and went out quietly into the hall. I could tie my shoes by feel.

I had my gun down one pant leg when I stiffly stepped outside. The sliding bolt had opened quietly. There was no one around to see as I walked with my one stiff leg past the dark dorm and down to the cow fence. Even the birds were still silent. It must be quite early. It wasn't easy to get through the barbed wire fence with one hand in my pocket gripping the gun to keep it from slipping. I limped down to the pasture until I couldn't be seen from the dorm, then I slid the gun out of my baggy pant leg and tightened my belt. The cows wouldn't tell if I went hunting.

The cows didn't seem to mind my disturbing them too much. They heaved heavily to their feet when I walked right at them, their breath blowing out intermittent clouds of white fog. The cow pies they made as soon as they stood up looked like they were steaming in the cold morning air. I blew out slowly. I couldn't make a white smoky colored donut in the air, but I could see my breath.

Down in the valley, the clouds made a sort of soft lake of white. The hills were still dark in the early morning. Even though I knew I shouldn't have snuck out, it was nice to be outside to see the sky slowly getting lighter as the sun chased away the fog in the valley.

I cocked my gun and left the barrel open. From my small hoard, I selected one out of the ten that were currently in my pocket, making sure the soft lead edges weren't dented. With the gun loaded, I headed down the steep hill into the valley, moving silently toward the sound of a Pin Tailed Wydah Bird. The little black and white males had a bright red beak and four long, narrow, black tail feathers. They liked to show off to the plain little tan and brown females by flying and dipping in the air above them, their long tail feathers making pretty little sweeping "S's" in the air. I wanted to get one if I could.

I had no idea what time it was when I headed back up the hill with no bird and no remaining pellets. The cows had scattered and were systematically biting off one mouthful after another of Kikuyu grass, swallowing without chewing. They would bring it up later to chew a few times when it was hotter. The cows were the only, living things around. I began to feel alone.

I also felt guilty as I again loosened my belt and pushed the gun down my pant leg, maneuvering carefully back through the fence. There was no one anywhere. I began to feel scared.

Maybe Jesus had come back and left me behind. The Bible said that he would come like a thief does, in the night, and that we wouldn't know when.

The Lord knew why my leg was so stiff. He said we needed to be ready when he came back, to abide in him, so that when he appears we may have confidence and not shrink from him in shame at his coming. He also said that we could be sure that everyone who practices righteousness has been born of him. Maybe I wasn't really born again.

Here I was hiding my gun down my pant leg. I had been out of dorm bounds for maybe hours. And hadn't I gotten up before the get-up bell, too? I knew God wasn't happy with me. He had come back, and I wasn't ready.

I heard some kids in the loquat trees. At first I felt a little better until I got closer and saw that it was only my roommates, Peter and Kenny. They didn't seem worried that Jesus had come back, and they were left behind too. I didn't want them to see me, so I continued walking stiffly towards the dorm. Somebody was coming out of the dorm. He didn't see me, but though he was the one I was hiding from, I was so happy to see him.

If Mr. Stauffacher was still here, I had another chance. I felt weak; I was so relieved.

The Bible reading is Matthew 24

Hunting With the Zandes

A Zande loves his gun. Once a barrel can be found, the rest can be made, provided welding is available somewhere. A water pipe stolen from the back of the missionary's house tends to split; maybe because it is stolen, but more likely because the black powder charge necessary to propel a 1/2 inch caliber ball is too much for pipe made in, and imported from, Kenya. Every dedicated Zande hunter knows that the tie rod, found connecting the steering arms between the front wheels of the missionary's car, is the perfect gun barrel. Hopefully there will be a rebellion soon and the car will be abandoned along the roadside somewhere.

The Zande culture is a hunting-gathering culture found in northeast Congo. Black powder and muzzleloaders came with the arrival of the Colonial culture, in this case the Belgians.

The Zande was quick to recognize the advantage of the muzzleloader in his own culture.

At Banda, Mr. Dix provided the welding services. Dr. Brown provided the surgical repairs necessary to the hunter after excessive enthusiasm during the loading process had produced damage during the discharging process. The Doctor's wife taught John 3:16 to all the patients awaiting surgery. "Bambiko Mboli akpinyemu aboro akpi zegeno dundiko, Ko afu gbangisa Wiliko, kasi guaboro asadi Ko, akpinga te, ankanyenye na ungani kindi." Because God loved all the people who are dying outside, He gave his only son… The missionary culture had come too.

The Doctor had a rifle, a 32-40: the lever action rifle with an octagonal barrel and a nine shot tubular magazine made famous in the Wild West culture of America. The Doctor also had a single shot, 20-gauge shotgun, an old 1929 Hercules model sold by Montgomery Ward. The Doctor used neither gun. The Doctor and his wife had a son who used the shotgun to hunt guinea fowl. The Zande and the son found a common cultural interest.

Mboligihe arrived at five in the morning ready to go hunting with me. It was quite a long walk to the peanut gardens where he had heard that the guinea fowl were digging up and eating the soft new peanuts. I had five shotgun shells in my jeans pocket. The Hercules on my shoulder, held by the barrel, pointed to one side of the path as we walked. Mboligihe had a machete. He would get one of the guinea fowl I hoped to shoot, and we would eat the others.

The path was beaten smooth and hard by many bare feet. Tall grass hanging across the path from both sides was wet with dew. Soon, Mboligihe's black legs glistened with moisture as he strode silently ahead of me. His shorts made hardly any sound; they were so soft and worn. My jeans were soon sopping wet below the waist and swished as I walked. Water seeped into my sneakers, and they squished with each step. Looking at the back of his shirt I marveled that the threads spanning the large holes somehow kept the sleeves where they belonged. The color of his shirt had long since adapted to its environment. He was the hunter, I the "Wiribawe."

The dew had dried, and the hot sun beat down. We had reached the peanut gardens some miles from the mission station, and there were no guinea fowl anywhere. However, they had clearly been here, lots of them, digging up the peanuts.

Mboligihe showed me the small Spirit Hut at the corner of the garden. It had been carefully made and resembled a miniature round Zande hut, no more than a foot high. The small conical roof was thatched carefully with soft grasses and showed no evidence of having leaked in the last rain. A few feathers, a bit of eggshell, a colored rock and a handful of rice, placed there to satisfy the spirits, remained undisturbed. Either the Spirits had been away or were unsatisfied with the offering because clearly the garden hadn't been protected.

The garden we had approached so carefully was left behind. Mboligihe was headed to another where he hoped the big birds had gone. I wondered if it was worth it. They must have eaten all they wanted and would now be looking for a soft dust bath somewhere. Cutting across a small ravine, we came to a clearing where there was evidence of someone having done a lot of work. Mboligihe said it was buda. We stood looking down at a half barrel, full of what looked to me like watery corn soup, or slop; it stunk. I knew the Zande worshipped the

SPIRIT OFFERING HOUSE

Spirits, but I didn't know what this half-barrel of liquid might have to do with worshipping Buddha. I thought he was a big, fat, gold, god in India somewhere. Mboligihe said, "Si begbrere gbhe!" I agreed. He dumped the barrel violently down the slope. It really stunk. We walked on.

Now the sun was high and very hot. The hunter wasn't tired, but I certainly was. Hunters never go home empty handed. As we kept walking, I watched the ripples of movement Mboligihe's muscles made in his back as he walked steadily ahead of me. His black skin was beaded with sweat where the holes in his shirt let his back show. I wiped the sweat again from my face with my sleeve.

Mboligihe sure didn't like Buddha, I thought, and he wasn't at all timid about dumping all that stuff down the hill. Here I was, a Missionary Kid, and I didn't even feel sure we should bother somebody who was making that stinking stuff for worshipping Buddha. I really should witness to this Zande. Maybe he believes in those Spirits and doesn't really know God. Mboli is the word for God in Pazande. His name means "God heard it," but that name is common among the Zandes. I kept walking, feeling the five shotgun shells still in my pocket and watching his back.

The sun was overhead. All the birds were quiet in the heat. I didn't know if Mboligihe had started back or not. We were just walking: that is, I was following him, and he was still hunting. Maybe if I prayed, God would send some guinea fowl. I could shoot one, and we could go home. My wet sneakers had dried out after walking a few hours in the hot sun, and now my feet were hot. With each step the back of the sneaker rubbed against what I was sure was a large blister.

"God, you could send some guinea fowl, if you wanted. I promise, if you do, I will give you all the credit, if I get one." My silent prayer was a bit desperate, but not too risky, cause guinea fowl hide down in the grass during the heat of the day. I guess I wanted a guinea fowl. I knew enough Pazande that I could have said something to Mboligihe, even as we walked. He walked; I trudged behind, watching his back.

KEE....

KE-KE-KEEEEE....

KEE....

KE-KE-KEEEEE!

The clatter of the birds, the beat of their wings as they flew from nearly under our feet startled both of us. We froze. We had apparently disturbed their dust bath! They never land in a tree at this time of day, but there they were, three of them in the trees, one nearly above us! The others dropped down into the tall grass and disappeared.

My heartbeat caused a rushing in my ears. My hands were shaking and sweaty, but the old Hercules gun still needed to be loaded. Pushing the lever slowly to the right to break the gun open, I tried not to let it click. The click was loud and sharp, but the great speckled bird just looked down and watched me push in the shell. The click when it closed wasn't so loud. Still the guinea fowl stretched his neck and looked down. The hammer clicked as I pulled it back fully. The bright brass bead of the front sight settled into line with the shallow groove near my eye, and the black silhouette of the bird against the sky.

The BOOM that shattered the noonday silence and the swishing thud of the bird two seconds later as it fell to the ground removed any thought of caution or silence. I rapidly forced the lever to the side and ejected the spent shotgun shell. The two other birds walked a step or two up their branches, looked at me, and stopped. I fumbled with the second shell in my excitement, but a few seconds later the gun roared again, and the second bird fell. The third guinea fowl was further away, out of range, so I started crashing through the tall grass towards it as I again loaded and cocked the gun. I stopped and fired. The third one hit a branch or two as it tumbled down into the tall grass.

Mboligihe was now leaping through the tall grass to the base of the first tree. Maybe the bird was only wounded with a broken wing and was running and flapping his way to freedom. I realized God must really have answered my prayer. The gun barrel was actually hot to the touch. I had never shot three at once before. I had to say something. God did it, not me.

"Merici fu Mboli," I yelled!

"Ee Bha, E Bha, Si kina wo. Ko du!" Mboligihe answered.

I had only said, *"Thanks to God."* Mboligihe had answered, "Yes, sir. Yes sir. That is the way it is. It is Him."

Mboligihe now held all three of the heavy guinea fowl, well fed on new peanuts. I watched as the drops of blood from their beaks made a bright contrast with the natural color on the back of his shirt. I think we both felt like hunters on the walk home.

Though I found out later, from my Mom, that buda in Pazande means beer, and that we had actually dumped a large supply of brewing potent home brew down the hill, I still can't forget Mboligihe's happy acceptance of the fact that it is God in our daily lives that makes things worthwhile. He didn't like Buda either. His Lord is also my Lord, though I can no longer hunt with Mboligihe.

After telling his prophet Isaiah that he was to go to the tribes of Jacob, God said, "I will **make you as a light for the nations, that my salvation may reach to the end of the earth.**" Jesus told us to be His witnesses even to the most distant part of the earth.

God's love and salvation is for every nation.

The Bible story is Matthew 7:24-30

I'll Never Tell

Young men, somewhere between 14 and 18 years of age, develop what are really rather normal, but definitely new, reactions to stimuli that have always been part of their lives.

Food had always been rather important, but now it takes on a completely new dimension! There is now never enough. Less than an hour after supper the young man who felt full and returned some leftover fried potatoes and bully beef to the pantry wishes that he had filled his pockets with bread. He is soon found scrounging in the room next door to see if they have anything to eat. This could be a real problem at Rethy, Congo because the dorm pantry was the only place food might be found at this time of night. A solution needed to be found.

Girls never used to be important at all, but now things are confusing. Boys had never before cared what girls talked about:

they were so silly anyway. Now however, they seem somehow disturbingly different, and it is necessary to develop a reliable source of information on just what they are thinking. What if she doesn't have a brother? Maybe he is just making up what he is telling you anyway. A way was also found to resolve this problem.

It involved the use of an Okapi pocketknife. They were sold at the dukas on a large, once colorful card, with ten or less remaining on display. The dusty card hung by one corner from a nail pounded into a shelf behind the store-width counter. It hung in front of shelves, which held matches, soap, sugar, salt, cloth and other bits of stuff, all out of the customer's reach. We and the Okapi knife manufacturers knew nothing about stainless or surgical steel blades, nothing about solid bronze sides fused to natural bone handles, nothing about knives equipped with hardened steel pivots and having a lifetime spring guarantee. The grinning duka owner assured us they were "muzuri sana," so the size and color of the soft plastic covering on the tin handle became the major negotiating points before the purchase was eventually made. Now we had a way to reveal the secrets of a girl's heart.

Breaking into the school at night wasn't allowed; at least I expect that is why Abrahamu was required to lock all the doors. But you need to understand that the girls invariably left valuable information in their desks. They couldn't help sharing and reacting to the knowledge that they were the subject of a new heightened level of interest on the part of the young men. Our surveillance of the girls became highly focused when the teacher's surveillance of us and of them faded. We thus had a good idea when a night entry would be the most productive. That's where the Okapi knife came in.

The Diamond brand sliding bolt lock on the back door was made in China. It was the school's fault it wasn't such a good lock. Also, they never replaced the long thin slat that somehow got broken. It was meant to act as a doorstop and to prevent access to the sliding bolt. It acted only as a doorstop. The long blade of the Okapi knife was inserted into the crack between the door and the door jam to cut against the bolt as closely to the left as possible, then twisted repeatedly to the right to slide the bolt open. If, by some remote chance Abrahamu had pivoted the bolt down to lock it properly, it had to be rotated as well as slid aside to open. The Okapi knife just needed to be pulled out slowly, in addition to the twisting procedure. Pulling the door more tightly closed to release the pressure on the bolt and oiling, or smearing it with butter the day before, made things easier. Locking the door on exit simply required the reverse procedure. The surface of the sliding bolt eventually became nicked after repeated entry. The knife blade became dull and rusty. The need to gather reliable information was satisfied. I never went, though I found the skill rather elementary. I never told. Nobody dared tell. The nighttime entries were never discovered.

Attempting to satisfy the other insatiable appetite I mentioned earlier required another expertise. The sliding bolts on the dining hall and pantry were made in the USA. The doorstop slats were made of Mbi and well nailed down. However, there was no ceiling in the pantry. The opening above the pantry was accessible from the attic above the dining hall. There was a ventilation opening to the outside on the other end of the dining hall. There was a decorative roof over the front door under the arched ventilation opening. There was a sturdy Golden Shower vine growing up the front of the dining hall, which had also spread over part of the roof. A small boy could fit through the opening. Left over bread and cakes were stored in the screen cupboards in the pantry. I think you can imagine what was done.

On the Friday night that the girls got permission to have a slumber party in the dining hall, it was found that the boys' two new compelling interests could be satisfied simultaneously. You see, the ceiling was very thin and girls apparently have slumber parties for something other than sleeping. I suspect that there were cracks in the ceiling because a lot was said, that I never heard, and very lengthy private discussions were held afterward by the boys involved. You see, I wasn't invited and some information is not to be shared with someone who might tell. I never told. They made quite a few trips to the pantry at night. They weren't caught for quite some time.

One night, preparations were made not long after the diesel generator was turned off. It was late, after 9:30 pm, and all was quiet except for the rustling in several rooms down our hall. One of my three roommates came very close to me and shown the dim orange light from his Tigerhead flashlight into my squinting eyes. He whispered threateningly in my face... "If you tell..., you'll get it..." I didn't move or blink. I just watched as they took dirty cloths and extra blankets and arranged them to make boy sized lumps in their beds. That was just in case the dorm parent came down the hall and shown his flashlight around to see if we were in bed.

They weren't all that noisy as they shushed each other on the way out, but the rubber strap on the end door was forgotten. For a change it closed the door, all by itself, with a bang!

I lay there and listened. It wasn't very long before I heard footsteps coming down the hall. Our door swung open. A brilliant flashlight beam stabbed around our room, probing each bed. My bed held the only realistic lump. My eyes were now tightly closed. I never moved. I said nothing. I would never tell. A short time later I heard the rubber strap on the end door do its job again, violently.

Should I have said anything? Was it wrong not to tell? Is it right to keep quiet? By kids' code, a tattletale's tongue is at risk of being split to become succulent tidbits for all the little puppy dogs. I still have my tongue. The Bible says:

"If anyone sees his brother committing a sin not leading to death, he shall ask, and God will give him life--to those who commit sins that do not lead to death."

It is quite clear that we are instructed to become involved if we see another Christian doing what is wrong. Certainly we are instructed to pray, not ignore him and let him head for death. The Bible also says:

"Brothers, if anyone is caught in any transgression, you who are spiritual should restore him in a spirit of gentleness. Keep watch on yourself, lest you too be tempted."

So don't just ignore those you know are doing wrong, and curl up in a little realistic ball of self righteous innocence under your old kaki army blanket, in your sagging cot. Maybe I should have said something to them.

The dorm parent caught them that night, though they heard him coming in time to hide with the skill of desperation. I don't know the details, but it seems one boy, whose nickname was "Apple," selected the oven as his hiding place. Rethy's ovens were then old 55 gallon steel barrels bricked in above a firebox. Bricks hold the residual heat for a long time.

Do you love your brother enough to do something when he is sinning?

Remember the oven.

The Bible reading is in Galatians 6:1-10

Searching for Treasure

Kids at a boarding school get to be pretty good at finding things to do in their free time.

There was no TV, no game boy, and no electronic games of any kind. In fact, there was no electricity unless the dorm parent started the diesel generator. The generator was run about four hours during the day, from 8 - 12 a.m., when we were at school and electricity was needed for the different departments at Rethy. It was run again for lights for three hours at night from 6–9 pm. There were table games like checkers, chess, Dominoes, and Parcheesi. We had a Carom table, but most of the caroms were lost. The Ping Pong paddles had lost their sandpaper faces, and our last Ping Pong ball didn't bounce very straight, even after we heated it in front of the fire to get the dent to pop out. It still worked, but the wrinkles left from the dent made it bounce funny. The girls liked to do puzzles and play Chinese checkers with the boys. It was mostly the biggie boys who seemed to like to play those games with the biggie girls.

We intermediates, liked to play outside games, if it wasn't raining. There were organized games we played together like softball, soccer, and volleyball or basketball, but those were a little too much like school. We had a field day too, but we organized our own games like Red Rover, Pom-Pom-Pullaway, Bachelors' button, Flying Dutchmen, and Three Deep. You needed to have lots of kids to play, and some were even more fun if the girls played. Prisoners Base and Capture the Flag, especially at night, were great fun. We had other group games like Winkum, Fruit Basket Upset, Musical chairs, and Magic Tricks we played inside if it was raining. There was one game that we could play day or night. That was Treasure Hunt.

Treasure Hunt would be popular for a while, and then we would forget about it until one of the teachers used it for the Saturday night activity; then it would become popular again. There were lots of ways to play. Usually there were hidden clues; sometimes there were treasure maps to figure out. The treasure was often candy, but it might just be the last clue saying your team had found the treasure and the candy was passed out at the dorm.

Years later, when I was one of the dorm parents, I recalled how much we had enjoyed the treasure hunts as kids at Rethy, and I decided to try to interest the kids. I made and hid a series of clues by sketching familiar places like the rope swing, the teeter tauter, the merry-go-round, the school sign, and the old bell Abrahamu rang every school day. I told the kids that there was at least 1/4th of the note showing if you looked at it from the right direction. I had found time to set up the two routes to the treasure hidden in the tree house while all the kids were in school Friday afternoon.

The kids loved it! The youngest kids looked in the cracks between the boards of the merry-go-round. They even crawled underneath to see if the clue was hidden under the roots of the Kikuyu grass that grew over the cement block there. The block held up the truck axel housing that was the center post of the merry-go-round Bill Stough had welded together from old truck parts, reinforcement bars, and angle iron. He was skilled in working with wood too and had built the platform with thick mahogany planks. It was a titchie who found the clue. They ran off towards the basketball backboards on the tennis court.

Picture treasure hunts became very popular. The kids made their own with the treasure just a sourball wrapped in a couple squares of TP, then in a page of paper from a school cahier. The drawings became very sketchy and kids took shortcuts to the popular, easy to sketch places hoping to find a quick route to the treasure. Though the hunt was fun, finding the treasure was best.

The best treasure hunt I remember as a kid was when Mr. Miller made a complicated treasure hunt where we had to figure out what place was referred to in a poem he had written, sort of like a code. The clues were hard to guess, and sometimes we even went to the wrong place to look for the next clue. Then we would study the clue again and get a new idea. We ended up running back and forth from one end of Rethy station to the other and back again, often passing the other teams going in opposite directions following their clues. It must have been a pretty evenly calculated course since all three teams ended up at the Miller's rose garden at about the same time.

All of us had had the same last clue, which was a poem about angles, distances, and how deep to explore below the lavender blush after gravity. We had all figured out it had to be different kinds of rose bushes, judging from the colors named in the poem, from which we had to measure the angles and distances. Actually the girls were very helpful on that clue. They even knew the names of the different rose bushes. The treasure had to be below the ground if it was that much further after gravity below a lavender blush. That must refer to a lavender rose. The only garden that had so many roses was the Miller's garden opposite their house down near the printing press. That made good sense too, since someone would have to watch to be sure the little African kids didn't dig up the treasure as soon as they saw Mr. Miller's garden man burry it for him.

We rushed there, only to find both other teams digging in the garden already. Our captain was Charlie Woodams, and he thought we ought to try digging wherever the soil was soft. We looked around for something to dig with. Some kids were using sticks and some just their hands. Mr. Miller was smiling, watching us cultivate his rose garden.

He must have gotten concerned that we would dig up his wife's roses because he stopped us. "OK," he said, "Now I want you to check the clue one more time and the three captains are to be the only ones to dig. Each is to make his measurements, choose his spot and dig straight down the distance he has calculated from the clue. If no one finds it, we'll have it dug up and shared with everyone."

The last team got to do their calculations first, but weren't to dig yet. I didn't think Charlie was careful enough when he made his measurements, but I kept quiet. I even agreed with the girls that the pink velvet must be the lighter pink, not the reddish one, but Charlie was the captain. David's team cheered for him and mocked Gordon when he measured for his team. David and Gordon's results were only about a foot apart. Charlie dug down as far as he had said he would. Nothing. My team had lost. David made his hole, and also found nothing.

No one thought Gordon would do any better, but he was down on his knees digging deeper than either of the other captains had figured. He thought the lavender blush measurement would start below a rose petal if it had fallen off, not from the beautiful lavender rose itself. Gravity would take a petal to the ground. His hole went a little crooked, probably because the dirt was softer there. He reached way down and didn't say much, but smiled. He must have felt something.

I never thought his team would win! They all got several Tootsie Rolls and some Sour Balls from inside the Oatmeal tin Gordon had dug up. The Tootsie Rolls were directly from the States, and they were so fresh even a sniff was a treat! Wow!

"He didn't dig straight down," someone on David's team complained. "He dug under our place."

"It is because his head sticks out in back that he is so smart," someone remarked. His head did stick out in back, but my ears stuck out and David Crossman's nose was different. We couldn't help it. Only a few guys looked as handsome as David and Bruce Weiss.

We used to think a treasure hunt was pretty special because of the treasure of course, but sometimes the treasure was something that didn't last very long at all. Even special Tootsie Rolls from America don't last very long. In fact, the sourballs from Kwandruma lasted longer. They didn't get stale either. The duka guy would even open the tin and you could pick any color you wanted, unless of course there were only a few white ones left in the sugar crumbs and chips at the bottom of the tin. A treasure worth something should last forever!

The Bible talks about that kind of treasure, worth selling everything you have in order to get it. The treasure in Jesus' story was found, not at the end of a trail of hidden clues, but sort of by accident when a man was plowing a field. He sold all he had to buy that field so the treasure would become his.

Read the Bible Matthew 6:19–22 and 13:44, 45

Camping on Mount Aboro

Mount Aboro, over 19,000 feet in altitude, dominates the northern end of the Blue mountain range in Congo. It was one of the favorite destinations for outings from Rethy. After the two hour hike up the hill, we would roll boulders down the steep rocky slopes and watch them crash through the trees as they made huge leaps, bursting with the fiery smell of flint and stone as they shattered. Flying kites was another favorite activity because a steady wind nearly always blew. Of course we usually took a picnic with us.

Today we had brought our stuff for an overnight on the mountain. We had no sleeping bags or special camping equipment so we improvised. My bedroll was my old khaki blanket rolled up really tightly and tied with string. So that I could brush my teeth at night like I was supposed to, I also

included my tooth-
brush and the small
collapsible aluminum
cup that I had gotten
from my dad. I guess
he had it in the army
years ago. The
concentric cylinders
fit loosely inside each

COLLAPSIBLE
ALUMINUM CUP

WITH
COVER

other when the cup was closed, but each had a slight taper so
they fit tightly together when pulled up making a small drinking
cup. I added my Tiger flashlight with the adjustable focusing
beam. I brought another tin can so I could heat up some water
to make myself some tea. It seemed like a good idea to bring
some extra socks so I put in one extra pair inside my rolled up
blanket. Now what else should I put in my bedroll? Maybe it
would be cold at night, so I added my jacket. I didn't know if I
would need a towel, but I brought one anyway. I could always
use it as a pillow.

I looked at what some of the other guys were bringing. It
seemed that food was something I had forgotten. They were
looking through the goodies they had gotten from home and
the stuff they had bought in the Dukas and hidden in their
bottom drawer. They put all kinds of things to eat inside their
bedroll. I didn't have any candy. All my cookies from home
were gone. My peanut butter was all gone too. I saw Peter put
in a couple of cans of condensed milk that he
had bought at the Dukas along with
a can of sardines. There was a
key attached to the top of the
can that you could use to peel
back the lid. A couple of guys
had bought some bully beef that
had a key on it too. A small tab of
metal on the side of the can
fit into the slot in the key.

CORNED BEEF

AUSTR

CANNED
MEAT

SARDINES
TO OPEN
WITH A KEY

- 83 -

You would then turn the key and continue on around the can until the strip of metal was ripped from the can and wound onto the key. Then the top of the can would be free. The corned beef came from New Zealand, but the guys bought it at the Dukas. Gary had an army surplus canvas covered canteen that he put into his backpack.

My backpack was really quite small, but I fashioned two loops of string around the bedroll and added arm loops so I could put it on my back and still be able to climb the mountain with both of my hands free. Some of the backpacks looked like they would fall apart before we got very far, but we were ready to leave right after school and all of us got into Mr. Stauffacher's light green International pick-up truck. We knew there was plenty to eat when we saw all the food that Mrs. Stauffacher had gotten ready for us.

The biggie boys had brought some iron bars along with them in order to dislodge rocks to roll down the hill. Every time we had a chance to climb Mount Aboro, we tried to find the loose rocks to roll down the cliffs, but some of them were just too big to move without levers.

Climbing up Mount Aboro could be extremely difficult during the rainy season. But if it were a clear day, the view would be beautiful when we reached the top. The ground was slippery where it had not yet fully dried, especially under the forest trees where it was damp and the ground was covered with moss.

The first part of the climb from where we left the truck was along the edge of corn gardens that had been made on the lower slopes of the mountain. The gardens were newly planted; it was open, and there were paths that we could follow up to the edge of the forest or grassland where it became too steep to cultivate. There was usually a hunters' trail that went up from the end of the gardens through the forest to the top of the mountain, so we looked for it. Some of the guys wanted to take a shortcut and go through the grass directly to the top, but that wasn't very smart. The grass and weeds and brambles were so intertwined that you just couldn't walk; you had to push your way and crawl around obstacles and over fallen trees. You might also come to a rock face that you couldn't climb and have to turn back.

The hunters' path through the moss-draped forest was longer, but it followed the ridge and was fairly easily passable. When we came out at the edge of the forest, we faced a long slope of bald granite rock that went the rest of the way to the top. You could look back down from an elevation of over 19 thousand feet to see the lines of Black Wattle trees that the Belgians had planted on either side of the few visible roads. There were also the different colored patches of disconnected gardens where the Africans had planted their various crops. There were then very few people that lived near Mount Aboro.

On the eastern side of the mountain that overlooked Lake Albert, from the top, we could see the lake shimmering in the distance. It was so clear that even the distant Uganda shore contrasted with the water surface. We searched the tops of the giant, Virgin-forest trees hoping to find the Vervet or the bigger Red Forest monkeys that might be feeding in the tree tops. It was no surprise to hear and see the croaking ravens objecting to our invasion of their domain.

In the area that Mr. Stauffacher had set up for his kitchen, each of us put the containers of food or water that we had carried up the mountain. Some of us hung around to help build the fire or do whatever chores he had in mind, while the rest headed off to explore. A couple of boys went on down the saddle to climb up the far peak where the ravens seemed to have their nest. Somebody was soon trying to make a kite. Paper airplanes were unsuccessful since there was too much of a breeze.

In the temporary puddles, left in the rock depressions after the rain, I found the strange plant life and the small swimming creatures fascinating. I wondered how they got there.

The guys with the iron bars went off in search of rocks that they could dislodge to roll down the slope. They would yell to let us know when one was loose and we would climb to a vantage point on the rocks to see what it would do to the forest on the Western slope. The thunderous crash, when the rocks dropped off a cliff and bounded into the air, was soon followed by the smell of sparks and pulverized flint that the breeze brought back to us. From the one boulder, several giant rocks bounded up from the impact and scattered into the trees below, some knocking trees down. Others were deflected and continued plowing a trail through the undergrowth on down the hill until they stopped. It was good nobody lived in that area at the base of the mountain.

We could see the clouds forming in the west as the sun set that night. The sunset was nothing special, and we began to wonder if maybe it would rain. After it got dark, the circles of flame and then the glowing coals on the end of sticks pulled from the fire made beautiful patterns as they were whirled around in the air. Mr. Stauffacher shared some thoughts from the Bible, prayed, and sent us off to the places where we had chosen to sleep in the open.

Part of the sky was pitch black and part was peppered with stars as I looked up at the night sky. The stars were slowly disappearing. It was getting cold. I put on my jacket and pulled the kaki army blanket up over my head. My mattress, made by the large ferns and the long grass I had cut and gathered made a fairly good cushion. The flat spot in the little rock hollow I had chosen was almost level. It was actually very comfortable.

I was awakened by a gentle rain and by the faint flickering of lightning followed by distant mumbling thunder. Pulling the blanket up over my head again and shaking off the droplets of rain helped for a while, but the rain steadily increased. The flashes of lightening were followed more closely by the rumble of thunder. After a particularly bright flash, I began counting,

1001... 1002... 1003.... Before I got to ten there was a definite boom of thunder. That discharge was less than two miles away! I was now getting wet from below, too, as my little hollow was apparently the drainage basin for the surrounding rock.

It began to rain in earnest. There was a bright blaze of lightning followed almost instantly by the roar of thunder. Even the mountaintop seemed to shake.

Mr. Stauffacher ordered us to get up immediately and roll up our stuff so we could get off the top of the mountain as soon as possible and return to the truck. He was making a fire since most of us were already drenched. Into a small cavity under the pile of small sticks he had gathered, he was carving off white curls of wood from a thick wet stick. The fluttering orange light from his small kerosene lantern was reflected in the black, wet, wood. He sloshed some kerosene from the lamp onto the wood and the damp carvings. He struck a match on the side of the box he had somehow kept dry. Union matches often just broke, fizzed hopefully, or even glowed brightly and failed to light the slender red matchstick as they flared up. Not this one. Mr. Stauffacher instantly put the flaring match against the kerosene soaked shavings. Soon we were warming ourselves, huddled around the hissing crackling fire.

The rain began to let up, and the lightning flashes seemed further away as the sound of the thunder followed faintly more than ten seconds later. Mr. Stauffacher must have had dry wood collected and covered just in case it rained. Before he went to gather everyone together he built up the fire arranging the wood so the water running off the top surface would not drip into the growing fire. Huddled under the ineffective shelter of our wet blankets, we were far from dry but were in no hurry to leave the fire that even the rain did not extinguish.

We were told to make up our bedrolls and that we would start down the mountain as soon as it was light enough to see. I'm sure there were items left behind as we packed up the best we could using our flashlights. My two red Eveready batteries with the big black nine and the cat picture on them still made the bulb glow a weak orange. Maybe part of the ninth life was still there, but I wasn't sure where the other eight cat lives had gone, nor could I find my toothbrush.

Bozo and a couple of the other oldest boys were to lead the way, and Mr. Stauffacher would follow in case anyone had trouble. We were all to take the hunter's trail. Keeping our footing was next to impossible on the slippery, black, muddy trail as we ran and slid or fell on our way down the mountain. When we gathered around the truck before heading back to Rethy, the evidence of those who failed to keep their footing was evidenced by the black, back-side of nearly every pair of jeans.

I didn't think much about the risk of being struck by lightning on the top of the mountain. I didn't think much before making my bed on the mountain in a little drainage basin. I didn't wonder how a fire could be made in the rain. I had my wet kaki army blanket, my wet jacket, and my extra socks- wet of course. My Tiger flashlight had Eveready batteries with no cats left. My toothbrush was lost. I'm sure that none of us thought much about all the filthy wet jeans we threw into the laundry box. Some of the first guys got hot, clean, water in the old tub and saved it for some guys who got lukewarm, grey water, who saved it for those who got something more nearly the color of what they were washing off. The towels ended up in the laundry box, some clearly having served to remove what was left after using the reused bathwater.

Mrs. Stauffacher knew we had to be hungry for our breakfast had been planned to be on the mountain. In the dining hall, hot slimy Oatmeal with the boiled milk from our own cows at the dorm tasted so good. The bread-toast was a little smoky, but the strawberry jam was great.

The sun came out, and there was still all of Saturday to enjoy. We were soon out on the wet grass playing soccer in a clean pair of jeans; jeans destined for the full laundry box by the end of the day.

Have you ever thought of the parents God gave you and how much they do to care for you? How much do we think is our right. The Bible says to obey and honor your parents. The parents are to be diligent in teaching their children of God and caring for them.

I had a dorm parent who shared the Bible on a mountain, built a fire in the rain, got us safely back home, and his wife fed us and cared for our filthy clothes, though my bath was rather cool.

The Bible reading is from Ephesians 6:1-4

Discovering Girls & Love

She loves me. She loves me not. She loves me…she loves me not. She loves me…. she loves me not. She loves me; she loves me not.

She loves me… she loves me not;

Now wait; I wonder if I should have started with "She loves me not." It looks like it might not come out right. Since ears of corn always have an even number of rows of kernels, maybe daisies always have an even number of petals. In that case, maybe the girls are right when they say it always turns out wrong because they always start with he loves me, and they always hope he does. It will turn out the same as what you started with only if there are an odd number of petals. Actually, if it is really up to the daisy to tell me if she loves me, I should not try to force the outcome should I.

She loves me, she loves me not; She loves me...

It's hard to figure out if she loves me from this silly old flower. Here is a petal that is only half as big. Maybe I shouldn't count this one.

We didn't really know much about love and not much about girls either. Sisters didn't count. We would get really embarrassed if we got teased about liking the girls. That meant we were sissies or that we might get cooties. I remember when one boy told me I liked a certain girl. I denied it and called her a "dumb girl." I said he said that because he liked her when actually I was hoping the daisy would help me solve my dilemma and tell me, "she liked me" because I kinda' liked her!

I thought I would like to show her how much I liked her. I made her a tiny little airplane. It was made out of Cypress scraps from the wood shop. I carved them with my pocket knife. The wing was cut from the thin veneer layer from a weathered piece of plywood, after being in the sun and rain. The wingspan was about three inches. I painted the plane red and white. I remember it being just about perfect. I gave it to her.

MY GIFT PLANE

Actually, I gave it to her brother. I think he gave it to her for me. She never said thank you, so maybe he kept it. But she still chased me in Pom-Pom Pull Away.

That was a good way to figure out if she liked me. Pom-Pom Pull Away was one of the games we could play with the girls. It was sort of like Tag, except you started with everyone on one side of the field and the "It" guy was in the middle.

When the "It" guy yelled,

"Pom-Pom Pull away, come away or I'll pull you away,"

everybody was supposed to run to the other side of the field and try not to get caught. If he caught someone, they were "It" too and stayed in the middle for the next time. The end lines were "Safe." You could pull someone off the safe line if they didn't come by themselves, but only the really brave guys would try to pull a girl off the safe line. I can remember chasing her in Pom-Pom Pull Away. She ran away really fast at first; until she sort of let me catch her, then she laughed. I liked to hear her laugh. I couldn't be sure of her feelings until *she* chased *me* when she was in the middle. If she chased me and I got away several times and still she didn't chase anyone else, then I could be quite sure she liked me. It isn't really catching, just tagging. Although according to the rules, maybe I could have tried pulling her off the base, but that was like holding hands. I was too timid to do that.

There was no game I liked more than Pom-Pom Pull Away when she came to play. There was no one I was more aware of or chased with such secret delight. When she chased me, I was ever so happy. She liked me.

I also teased another little boy, saying he liked her. That was to help keep my special secret. Of course he objected, but he made such a big deal about it that I got jealous. That clearly proved that he also liked her. Two little boys were talking about a cute, brown haired girl, boys that such a short time ago knew only that girls had cooties and were to be totally avoided.

Our relationship progressed, and I made her another gift. This one was a little carved fish, like the leaping trout on the cover of the tattered Boy's Life Magazine I found in our boys living room. It was two inches long, made of corkwood, and fastened to a little plaque. I painted it silver and gray. Her brother gave it to her for me.

I was now bold enough to wink at her in our Winkum games. In Winkum we set up the chairs in a circle, with the girls in the chairs and a boy standing behind each chair. If there weren't enough boys, one boy took care of two girl chairs. There had to be an extra empty chair in the circle with a boy behind it too. The guy with the empty chair would wink at the girl he wanted to come to his chair, and she would try to escape from the boy guarding her chair. If he could tag her before she got off the chair, she had to come back. If the girl tried really hard to come when you winked at her that was a good sign. If some girl just sat in your chair and didn't try to leave, that might be good or bad. If you liked her, that was good, but how could you see if the girl you liked would try to come to your chair if you never got an empty chair in front of you. When I finally got her in front of me, I held my hand so close to her that I could tell she was warmer than my hand. She flipped her hair around and looked back at me when I tapped her. She said, "Who winked at me?" She was laughing, and her hair smelled so good I could only grin real big, but I kept my hand close. I could see Peter winking at her, but then, he winked at all the girls.

Things were nearly perfect. I was learning lots about girls, but I can't remember ever saying anything much to her. I certainly was never bold enough to tell her that I liked her, or to ask to hold her hand.

We had another game we played that was most helpful in our discovering girls. In Flying Dutchmen you had to start in a big circle with everyone holding hands. It usually started with all the boys on one side and the girls on the other with the circle completed between brothers and sisters. Two were left as the Flying Dutchmen outside the circle. They ran around in one direction, and tagged between two kids where their hands were joined. Then there was a race. The two who were tagged ran around the circle the opposite way, trying to return to their place before the Flying Dutchmen got there. Of course there was often a crash when the four met on the far side of the circle. The first to fill in the open spot would join hands with the rest of the circle, and the other couple became the Flying Dutchmen. It was soon easy to tell which gal was a favorite of which guy since, if you were fast enough as a Flying Dutchman, and picked the couple on the correct side of the girl you liked, you could end up next to her, holding hands. She had a soft hand.

By college I had progressed considerably in my expression of affection. Actually I was rather skilled. I soon discovered her name from the Bird Dog Book of all the new freshmen. Her schedule was available at the registrar's office, and it was easy to calculate her route between classes using the map of the campus. My routes became considerably longer than before my research, but we crossed paths rather frequently. I tried smiling, but she may not have noticed.

I decided that a little Love Bird might be an appropriate gift. I fashioned the 1 1/2 inch form out of melted plastic and in their proper places I glued the tiniest colored feathers from the preserved skin of a red-headed lovebird from Congo. She was from a place called RVA in Kenya and would surely like it. It was exquisite. I put it on cotton in a small jewelry box. I didn't give it to her brother.

By cutting across a row of seats and working towards the front of chapel, I managed to give it directly to her as she left chapel. The next day she said thanks, but she never wore it. I wonder what she did with it.

It seems my gifts were to be rather ineffective. How do you really express love to the one who means the most in the world to you? How did I ever get a wife, anyway?

By the way, how do you express love to God?

God told Amos that He hated their feast days, the solemn assemblies, the gifts, and the offerings. He told them he wouldn't accept them. He told them to take away the noise of their songs, that he wouldn't hear the melody of their instruments.

God said, "to do what he wants us to do is far better than anything we have to give him."

So, how do you tell God you love Him?

You deny yourself and follow Him. You make yourself the servant of all, like He did.

It doesn't seem that making a little plane, a corkwood fish or even an exquisite tiny, feathered lovebird did much good in my courting efforts. Giving God your stuff doesn't help much either. He's not broke. Do what he says.

I did get a wife! WOW. We got to know each other. We did an old fashioned thing, called writing letters. In fact we each wrote over 700 letters to each other. Ever thought of reading God's letter to you? Once you know God, you want to give Him everything. It is His anyway, but He likes it when we do things His way. I did carve my fiancé an ivory rose, but she never wears it since the red velvet dress with the rose on it was lost when we evacuated from Zaire. She always wears a small diamond ring, though. I sold my car to buy it.

Give God yourself.

The Bible reading is in Matthew 7:21-27

She Was Cute

She was cute from my eighth grader's point of view. Her hair was brown and curly. She had brown eyes too. Her brother was my best friend. She could run really fast in Pom Pom Pullaway, and I thought she might have chased me a little more than she chased the other guys, but I wasn't sure. She had a cute little straight nose. I was well aware that mine turned up at the end. My hair wouldn't lie down properly, and besides it wasn't black. I wasn't "tall dark and handsome" or "wide in the shoulder and narrow at the hip." I wished I was... so maybe then she would like me. I had had her brother deliver some gifts I made for her.

I could carve better than any of the other kids, and I almost wanted to keep the little plane I made for her. I heard she had it on her dresser, so I'm sure the other girls asked from whom it came. I hope she liked the little fish carved from the corkwood I had found in the pine forest at midterm.

I thought maybe she liked me a little bit since she didn't seem to mind when I ended up beside her in Flying Dutchmen, or when I caught her in Bachelor's Button

Then... one day her brother came up and secretly told me, "My sister likes you!!"

"I'm on the, top of the world,

looking down on Creation

and the only explanation I can find;

is the love that I've found,

ever since you've been around,

that has put me on the top of the world."

I still like that song even though I have no idea who made it up. That's what I felt like!

I was on the top of the world! She was the only one I could see! Even the sky was bluer than usual. We chased each other in Pom-Pom Pull Away. I shamelessly winked at her in Winkum and tried to work things so I might sit by her in Fruit Basket Upset or hold her hand in Flying Dutchmen. I chose my seat in study hall so I could see her from behind my propped up book. I even winked at her during study hall ... and she winked back. At the box social, I won the bid for her lunch, and we ate together. Peter made me bid really high before he quit bidding. Even though I couldn't think of much to say, she seemed to like it. All was well.

I remember not minding anymore that I was just *me*. She liked me! She liked me the way I was, even though I wasn't the tallest, the fastest, or the strongest boy in the dorm. My hair was blonde and didn't lie down very well. It tried to curl if it got long. But she didn't seem to mind. Her brother said she liked me, so she did! I was on the top of the world.

Then... a few months later ... I was crushed. During study hall one evening I saw the sparkle of something in her curly brown hair, near her ear. She had seemed so perfect, but now she was wearing an earring. Only worldly girls wore earrings. I couldn't wink at her. She hadn't smiled back at me in Bible class when I had smiled at her. I was confused. Study hall was three times as long that night.

On the way out of study hall I walked as closely behind her as I could. I looked carefully and discovered that what I thought was an earring was just a loose bobby pin, but the magic had dimmed. She seemed in a hurry to leave the dining room and get back to her dorm.

Her brother was best friends with another boy, Peter, and she chased Peter in the games we were allowed to play with the girls. I knew Peter liked her, but she was still nice to me. I went quietly back to my dorm room.

Then, later that night, just before lights out Peter, Kenny, Lester and Gary burst into our room. They collapsed on Peter's saggy bed and pulled out some small scraps of paper and began looking through them. I guess they had been to school again to see what they could find in the girls' desks.

"Listen to this," Peter said as he gleefully read from a small pencil written note. "I have so much fun with _ _ _ _ _. I like him so much." No matter how I tried, my name P, A, U, L, would not fit in the five blanks. They were reading notes from Mary Anne's desk, and she was my girlfriend's best friend. Now I knew for sure. The world I had been on top of, fell in on me.

What was it back then in eighth grade at Rethy that somehow convinced me that my failure to be "tall, dark, and handsome," or "broad at the shoulder and narrow at the hip" greatly reduced my chances of being liked by a certain girl? What made me so distressed at the sparkle I saw near her ear?

What made me "tear unheeding through the thorns, and climb fearlessly the highest rocks in Rocky Pine Forest?" What made me "feel my life worth nothing" when she liked _ _ _ _ _ instead of me? Wasn't it a system, or systems of values, that I had absorbed in my life in the boarding school for MK's, through reading a couple Zane Grey novels, listening to preachers, or watching the other kids at school? There certainly wasn't any TV in Congo, but there was "worldly" music. We watched no movies; they were "worldly" of course. There were no adds, no magazines, and no newspapers, but the MK's recently returned from the States seemed to know. Even what we wore could be right or wrong according to some set of values.

Where do those values come from? In tempting Jesus, the Devil offered all the power over all the kingdoms of the world for the power had been given to him. He is also called the Prince of the Power of the Air. His influence is certainly involved in establishing this set of values that we call the world.

The Bible says, "the world is passing away along with its desires, but whoever does the will of God abides forever."

I guessed that I wasn't good enough for any of the girls. I wished I could be like Jonathan or Wetzel in the Zane Grey book I had read, except that I was rather ordinary. I did climb the highest rocks in the forest that day. I wandered far from the group who was gathered around the big fire where the picnic was being set up. Lots of the kids' parents had come for the event. There was lots of shouting, and most of the bigger boys and girls were playing volleyball with some of the parents. They had stretched a net across the main road, as that was the most level spot. Cars came so rarely that that caused no problem. After a while I couldn't hear them anymore. Maybe I was lost. It was a huge forest. I partly hoped I was lost.

I found some good corkwood on a tree far
from the road. I broke off a
piece and began carving a
small rowboat. The soft
yellow wood curled
up away from my
knife. I chipped
out the interior of
the boat even re-
moving the wood under the seats. My knife was very sharp.
Eventually the tiny yellow chips had covered my lap and were
scattered on the soft bed of Cypress needles around me. I made
the sides of the boat ever thinner. It was now almost perfect
and very fragile.

It was getting cooler in the forest. The afternoon sun was
behind the hill. I hadn't thought about eating, but it must be
late now. I didn't want to have them looking for me as they
would ask why I went off away from everyone. I had better try
to find the truck. I put the delicate little yellow corkwood
rowboat in my shirt pocket.

Someone with five letters in their name had stolen the girl I
hardly talked to, the one who now was talking with her so freely
just a few feet away in the back of the dorm truck. We were
standing, packed in rather closely together, trying to keep our
balance on the bumpy roads as we were driven back to the dorm
after our mid-term picnic.

When we got back to the dorm, there were only chips of
thin yellow corkwood in my pocket.

The Bible reading is 1 John 2:15-17

The First Step

I remember when we were told that we had taken the first step. We joked around about the first step, but I think Mr. Stauffacher was serious when he warned us that we had taken the first step.

We all knew he was talking about something between boys and girls, and having taken the first step we were much more likely to do something we shouldn't do. I think he was referring to a very bad thing, but frankly I wasn't very clear on what he was talking about. I guess I was just ignorant about some things. He said this was too special a thing to take lightly. I guessed it was something very serious and there were several steps before it was really bad.

I am sure some of the boys knew what he meant. I hadn't been in on the secretive talks some of the boys had down at the cattle dip, hiding between the walls that kept the cows in line as they were driven into the dipping tank. It was a place no one could easily see them or hear them. They put someone to watch to see if anyone was coming. They didn't want the dorm parents to know they were just talking about girls and stuff down at the dip. The cows had gone through long ago, but they stayed to listen to Jacob Englebricht. He seemed to be the one who knew lots about girls. He wasn't an MK. His Belgian parents were coffee plantation owners and wanted him to get an education at our school in English.

I was in ninth or tenth grade at the time. I remember that girls were becoming sort of mysterious and very interesting, something I hadn't realized before. We always had a devotions time in the dorm parents' apartment living room after supper, just before study hall. If we were completely quiet, we were allowed to come in as early as we liked after supper. We could sit and look at National Geographic Magazines and listen to music. Mr. Stauffacher liked classical music and usually had it playing while he sat there and also read. He was usually reading his Bible or preparing for the classes he taught at school. The Stauffachers had both girls and boys in their dorm, the girls down one hall and the boys down the other with their apartment in between.

I liked the Stauffachers. We always called him "Mr. Stauffacher." I remember that he was a strict, fair, honest, Godly man, one who was a hard worker and enjoyed his work. I'm not sure when he began his day, but he used to have personal devotions and even found time to fix watches from time to time before he woke us in the morning. He was in charge of the biggie dorm, the workmen, the building of the auditorium, and at the same time the principal of the Academy. He taught all day and supervised the evening study hall. He was often in the carpenter shop working on new desks for the school. For relaxation he worked in his private garden where he even grew sweet corn, Golden Bantam, if I recall correctly.

As soon as he dismissed school, he was off on a several hundred-mile trip to Napopo where he would teach the Azandes in the Bible school during the break.

When we asked his permission for any one of a number of activities only MKs can invent, he would answer briefly and usually predictably, as the answers were consistent. It was no use to beg or ask again or send someone else with the same request, hoping for a different answer; it would be the same and it wasn't always "no." When he said something, we could count on it completely; when we were disciplined, we deserved it. His Bible lessons at school were practical and applied to what we were doing every day. The Bible was completely trustworthy, and if the Bible said it; that was the way it was. His life was such that we knew he knew God. The Stauffachers were very careful about the interaction between the boys and the girls. Even the area outside the dorm was divided into the areas for the girls and the guys. The brick path down the middle of the front lawn that led to the road was the boundary in front of the dorm. I remember dividing a package from Mom and Dad with my older sister on that path. There were certain common paths to the dining room and school, but generally the boys and girls were kept separate.

The Stauffacher's living room thus had an extra attraction. The girls often came in early, well certain ones I guess, and some of the guys came in early too. Certain ones, that is. It wasn't only to listen to classical music and look at pictures of animals in the National Geographic. I had a certain interest in going in early – if some other guy would go in too, that is.

Now there was one more rather special event. You probably wouldn't think it very special. But, on Sunday we were allowed to go for a walk, a girls' and boys' walk that is. It worked something like this. The girls walked in a giggly group, and the boys walked in another, occasionally sneaking ahead to jump out from behind a large Cypress tree trunk. It was to scare the silly girls, they said. Only the bold boys, like Peter, did such things. Maybe there was something going on and they wanted the girls to notice them. The Stauffachers would walk with us, usually somewhere in the middle of the group. We usually took the walk in the afternoon after our English church service and before supper. After supper on Sunday there wasn't much to do.

Well, the event that led to our being admonished about having taken the first step happened on a Sunday evening. We somehow got the Stauffachers to agree to let us go for a walk at night. We were to get our flashlights and stick together. It was about 1 and 1/2 miles around the loop, down the hill on the road from the dorms between the Jacaranda trees towards the cattle dip. There followed the road beneath the tall Eucalyptus trees, which shaded the road from the moonlight, making a long, dark tunnel towards the main road. The bright white or orange dots of light from our flashlights darted around often shining at the girls ahead of us. They would laugh as they turned and told us to mind our own business.

Peter disappeared. Lester was the best at sneaking ahead and hiding behind the trees. He liked Mary Anne. It seemed that quite a few of the boys had other ideas than just walking on this particular Sunday evening. I am sure it was just innocent fun. The guys climbed the steep banks off the main road and, hiding behind the striped cactus plants, ran ahead along the barbed wire fence. They came out ahead of the girls when they returned to the road from one of the dry drainage ditches. Things started getting mixed up, and the number of girls ahead of us seemed to be fewer.

After climbing the hill in front of the school, taking advantage of the shortcuts across the cow pasture, by the time we got back to the dorm I was very sure we had lost quite a few guys and maybe some girls along the way.

We all knew pretty well who liked whom since they winked at each other in Winkum, chased each other in Bachelor's Button, and managed to end up beside each other in Fruit

Basket Upset. Somehow the same thing happened in Flying Dutchmen with the same couples ending up beside each other holding hands in the circle around which the "Flying Dutchmen" had to race to get to the empty spots. I knew how to do it too. If your racing couple reached the opening in time, and the girl whose hand you wanted to hold reached out towards you, it was a very good sign. If she appeared not to notice, well, that wasn't so good. Now, several of the known couples were missing.

Mr. Stauffacher had very little to say when we got back in the dorm. A couple of kids stayed in his living room to read National Geographic magazines, but most of the rest of us went down our halls. It was almost lights out time. But the lights stayed on.

Mr. Stauffacher was never early or late shutting off the lights. He always came down the hall at five minutes to nine and blinked the lights by using the lever on the switch box at the end of our hall. Many of us had no watches. We knew that in five minutes we had to be in bed and the lights would go out. At exactly nine o'clock he would return and the lights would blink out when he pulled down the lever and locked the end door with a sliding bolt on the inside. When the lights went out, I could hear the diesel motor in the shed out back momentarily pick up speed and then resume the steady tone we hardly noticed. He would let the motor run another half of an hour before shutting it off. Then all would be quiet and dark. But tonight the lights stayed on.

The rest of the guys finally came in the end door wondering why the lights were still on. There was lots of whispering. Where were you guys? I think I heard someone talking about kissing, but I probably heard wrong. They were getting ready for bed very quickly and rather quietly, in spite of the subdued whispers of excitement.

Then the bell went. Mr. Stauffacher was ringing the bell that he rang for devotions, or to wake us up. We knew we were supposed to come to his living room, even though it wasn't the normal time. We obeyed. Some got dressed again. Some quickly got in their PJs and pulled on a robe. Some of us got out of bed and pulled on our robes. The girls would probably be there too. They were there.

Mr. Stauffacher gave us a talk about taking the first step and told us we had to read Psalms 31 and 51. What was the first step? Was he right?

The Bible reading is in 2 Samuel 11:1&2

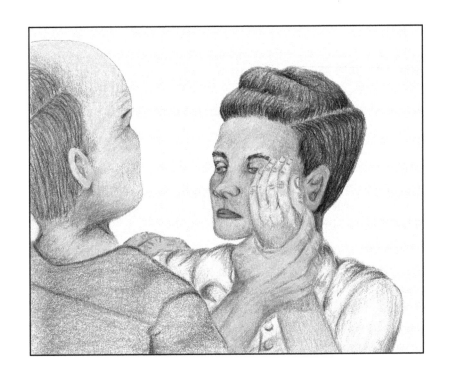

Go Jump in the Lake

Sunday mornings were different. The dorm parent came down the hall fifteen minutes later than usual, ringing the small dented hand bell to wake us up. He didn't bother to ring it in every room. As usual, we were expected to read our Bibles and pray during the fifteen minutes of quiet time, but, as usual, most of us just rolled over or kept on sleeping. We were so used to the bell. Some guys got up and went to the bathroom so they could use the left over hot water that had been heated for the baths on Saturday, if any was left. After fifteen minutes the second bell rang from just inside the door at the end of the hall nearest to the dorm parent's apartment. We had another half hour to get up, get dressed, make our beds, clean our rooms, and do our jobs before breakfast. That meant we could sleep 25 more minutes because Sunday's were different; he didn't come check to see if we were getting up.

My white nylon crinkle crape shirt from Montgomery Wards was still dirty from last Sunday, so I got up to wash it. I wished I could just throw it in the wash, but Mom said they would wreck it. They would try to iron it, and it was this special sort of see through stuff that didn't need ironing. The charcoal iron was usually too hot for nylon and a coal would burn a hole in it if it fell out of the vent holes in the iron. So, I washed my shirt with yellow Sunlight soap in the sink, rinsed it twice, and then rolled it up in my towel to get it to dry. It was so thin; it was nearly dry when I put it on over my best undershirt, the one with no stains in the front.

Sundays we also had to wear our leather Sunday shoes, and they needed to be polished. Some guys had a polishing kit with applicator brushes, polishing brushes, and buffing blocks for brown and black. I just used an old sock wrapped around my finger to smear the black Kiwi polish on my shoe. If I spit on the sock first and rubbed for a long time after smearing the polish on, I could get a real spit shine. Rubbing the toe of the left shoe on the back of the right pant leg, and the right shoe on the back of the left pant leg, just before entering the auditorium for Sunday school, removed any dust that accumulated on the way.

We also had our offering money. With the clothing list showing where to sew in the name tags, Rethy Academy sent a recommendation for each child to be given 60 franks for Sunday school offerings and 40 franks for spending money. Some kids got 500 franks for spending money, but my Mom sent exactly what they said in separate labeled envelopes. The Dorm parents kept the money for us. We could get spending money from them on Saturday to use in the dukas or to spend on candy at the school canteen. On Sunday, we had to get our 5 franks each week from the dorm parents just before we went to Sunday school. I put my offering in, but lots of the guys just put their hand over the basket with nothing, or dropped in a few centimes left over from Saturday and kept the offering money maybe to buy a live little bird from some African kid. The dorm parents gave out the money and also counted the offering. I'm sure they knew what was happening, but they couldn't know exactly who was keeping the offering, except maybe the guy who had the bird?

Well, this particular Sunday, I got my money in the rush with the other guys at first; at least I am quite sure I did. It was nearly time to go to Sunday school. Some of the guys had gone already, probably to walk with the girls who always left early.

Gary was coming down the hall, nearly to the end where I was and yelled at me, "Ma Crossman says to come get your offering money."

"Aw, tell her to go jump in the lake," I responded. "I already got it."

That *that* wasn't a good thing to say was immediately obvious. That I had said it loud enough to be heard at the other end of the hall was also apparent. That Mr. Crossman was there with his wife was not that unusual. He liked her a lot, I guess. A very strong, masculine voice thundered down the hall. "Paul Brown, you come here immediately!"

Now, maybe I should tell you a little about Mr. Crossman. He was strong. He was very strong. He was exceptionally STRONG. He could put a 55 gallon barrel of fuel up on a pick-up truck all by himself. His neck was so strong that he could lift a sack of grain with only his teeth. He pushed down a brick pillar. I saw it. His hands were thick and calloused. He grew up on a farm, working all the time. He was usually quite quiet, but now he had yelled at me. "You come here immediately!" I didn't dare disobey.

There were a couple of other kids there. I went to stand in front of him. His wife was there at a small table where she was writing down the offering money she gave each of us that morning. He looked me right in the eye. His voice wasn't as loud any more, but I could tell he was extremely upset with me.

I just looked back at him; I didn't feel guilty for not getting my money.

He said, "Did you say that?"

I just replied, "Yes."

"Apologize!"

"I'm sorry."

Instantly I was on the floor, my head ached, my cheek stung. I knew he had slapped me on the side of the head. My eyes were burning, tears I didn't want any of the kids to see were sliding out of the corner of one eye towards my ear, and the other eye was making a tiny puddle next to my nose. I sniffed and got up and went down the hall. One of the guys asked, "What happened?" and I wouldn't answer. I went to Sunday school.

I had peeked in the mirror at my cheek, and it had a raised red welt that matched the powerful hand that had hit me. The guys seemed to think I was some sort of brave hero. But I wasn't. I didn't want any of the girls to see. I entered Sunday school with my hand trying to cover the large mottled red handprint on my face. Mr. Crossman came up behind me, tapped me on the shoulder, and motioned me to follow him outside. Almost gently, he took my hand down from the side on my face to see the handprint he had made. I think he felt sorry that he had hit me so hard, but I don't remember what he said. Somehow I knew that he wasn't angry with me anymore.

Why did he hit me? Did I deserve it?

At the time I didn't think so. I hadn't done anything wrong. I had given my offering the way I was supposed to. I hadn't meant her to hear me tell her "to go jump in the lake." I certainly hadn't expected him to hear me. After all, I just said it to Gary. What I said didn't mean anything to me.

Now, I see things a lot differently. I was a proud cocky kid, trying to look tough before the guys. I refused to cry, even if my eyes did leak a little. I had looked right back at him before he punished me. I had pretended it didn't hurt when they asked me. I wanted the girls to think I wasn't hurt, hiding what clearly must have hurt. I was proud.

Now what I said didn't mean much to me, but the Bible talks about a Lake of Fire where are to be cast the beast, the false profit, the Devil and his angels, death and hell, and those whose names are not written in the Lamb's Book of Life where they will burn with fire and brimstone forever and forever. In a way I told Mr. Crossman's wife "to go to Hell." I showed no respect for those in authority over me. It was more important for me to look good before the other kids in the dorm, especially the girls.

I thought I had all the answers. I *did* nothing wrong, but I was proud. Pride is thinking of yourself as more important than you are. The Bible says pride comes before destruction and a haughty spirit before a fall.

We are told "not to think of ourselves more highly than we ought to think; but to think soberly, according as God hath dealt to every man the measure of faith."

The Bible reading is in Proverbs 6:16–19 & James 4:10

A Drink of Water

When we hiked to the lake, it was as hard as climbing a mountain. You might call it a negative mountain; we went down. What goes up must come down, right? And what goes down must come up. Well, we went down and had to come up again.

Our mountain, actually a plateau, was where we lived at Rethy, about 7,200 feet in elevation, and we went down to Lake Albert, elevation 2,000 ft. That's a lake, a mile low, and Kilimanjaro is a mountain, two miles high. The hike up Kilimanjaro was, I understand, hot to cold, back to hot, while Albert was cold to hot, back to cold. That's sort of a negative mountain, right?

We started at about 5:30 in the morning from Nioka Foret, nearly running down the well-beaten path. It was so steep that it was impossible to walk easily. It was just light enough to see with the early rays of the morning sun splitting the sky. The sun was white. Maybe it would be hot. We were full of energy. After a mile, it was too steep to run and there were big irregular steps down, one worn foothold to the next. We zigzagged from one side of the path to the other, around rocks and damp depressions in the path left from the puddles after the rain. There were two miles of easy stuff and then it became yet steeper. If I slipped, I grabbed at the long grass beside the path or ended up sitting on the muddy spot, my feet hanging out over the next step. Going backwards was the least risky at those slippery places. Far below, the palm trees around Ngenge could be seen, tiny balls on bent stalks. The people resembled colorful ants flowing in on various trails then mingling in the center, the market place that was on a miniature soccer field.

There was loose rock on the path now and no thought of running. I looked at the view. The blue of the lake and sky merged together in the distance, the sun glaring brightly and the lake full of silver reflections. My legs trembled and felt hot from all the jolting, and it was easy to stop and look, but not so easy to start again. I could see specks of kids back up above me, but Pete Epp was catching up, so was Gary Kline, and Danny Nelson was with them. Ken Schuit was way back. I wanted to be first.

I was first to Ngenge, the plateau where the busy market was in full session. Now my knees felt as if the joints were watery, not too well attached to whatever that was down below. It felt as if there were blisters starting, but I didn't dare look. I had to stop and wait. I didn't know where to go next. The guys were catching up. When Pete arrived, he started asking the way. We began walking. We hadn't seen Mr. Crossman since we left the truck at the top of the hill.

A tenth grader's legs recover quickly, and we were soon passing one another on the fairly even grade for the next few miles. It felt good to climb a small rise from time to time. The thigh muscles that put on the brakes had had a real workout. Cooling hot feet as we crossed small streams felt good, but walking in wet sneakers didn't help the blisters any. We passed another palm-shaded village and were shown the next path that led down to the lake. Our steps had slowed; I was no longer looking at the scenery but at the ragged sweaty back of the little African boy in front of me. He said he knew the way. We hadn't seen the lake since before Ngenge, but when the lake again came into view there were dugout canoes on it, scattered around near the shore like floating matchsticks. Our goal was near, yet still so far! I was able to get ahead again after we stopped for water at a stream.

Now there was no shade. There were no men carrying fish up to the market place. No one was going down the path but us. My little guide had stopped at the stream. It was just too hot a time of day for reasonable people to travel. The tall dry grass made small cuts in my hands when I had to grab it to keep from falling. I became more and more conscious of my goal and noticed my blisters less and less. The lake below was now so close it filled the entire horizon, a deep blue against the blistering white sky.

I stood on the shore. All was quiet except a gentle lapping of the water at the edge of the great lake. There was no activity in the fishing village a short way off. Several black Kites circled lazily around looking for fish entrails floating in the water left from the cleaning of the night's catch. They would swoop down and pick the pieces neatly off the calm surface of the lake and pick at them slowly in their circling flight.

Pete came, nearly running towards the water, his shirt already off, his pants on their way, and somehow kicking off his shoes, he rushed into the still lake water. I followed his example, well sort of. I left my stuff in a neat pile then waded into the clear water. Looking down with the water at chest level, I could nearly count my toes, if I was very still.

I don't remember eating my lunch, by then a wad of bread, peanut butter and jelly, with roast beef slices all mashed into the corner of the plastic bag. My drinking water was gone. The sun was directly overhead.

"To get back to the truck, we have to get started," said Mr. Crossman. He had finally arrived, very red in the face. He was the strongest man I knew, and I didn't quite understand what took him so much longer to get there.

The goal to be first was not important on the way back. The pace was slow. The air was still. Before long we were all wet with sweat. I repeatedly wiped my face on my sleeve. Some of the guys took their shirts off. Before we reached the top of the first steep climb, I was so hot there was no sweat to dry off my face. There was nothing I wanted more than water. At the stream where we had cooled our feet on the way down we all put our faces in the water and sucked up water the way a cow does. My water bottle would no longer hold water. Falling on it hadn't helped the integrity of its structure, so I left it with a little African boy by the stream.

Refreshed, we were again on our way. Mr. Crossman and the rest of the guys were somewhere behind us, maybe a long ways. An hour of hiking later, at Ngenge, we faced the two long steep hills, to the top. It was the hottest time of the day. The shrilling insects that are normally a continuous background of noise were silent in the heat. The people at Ngenge sat totally still, just talking, in the dense shade of the mango trees or on low benches under the eaves of their huts. We started up.

Earlier we had been extremely hot and tired. Earlier we had been thirsty. Those were superlatives two hours ago, now they were only comparatives. Before, we had had a stream ahead, now there was another mountain slope in the beating afternoon sun. My heart was racing, a rushing sound in my ears. I couldn't even spit. We were near the top of the first half and Danny was digging, less efficiently than a dog, but in a similar manner, in what had been a damp spot in the path. Pete and I watched hopefully. We desperately wanted a drink.

Can you make a productive borehole in a damp spot in a path on the side of a mountain with your bare hands? Apparently not. Even Danny gave up. We went on.

A woman met us at the top of the first steep slope. Her house was nearby, she said. I have never had better water to drink. I drained the first half sufferia without a pause. She laughed and went and got some more. That time I noticed the taste, delectable! I'm sure it wasn't boiled, though it did taste faintly of smoke. It wasn't cold, but nothing has ever been more refreshing.

Jesus said, "For truly, I say to you, whoever gives you a cup of water to drink because you belong to Christ will by no means lose his reward."

I remember thinking that that happy woman will have a great reward. It was the same as giving a drink to Jesus.

That is what he said, isn't it?

How long has it been since you did something for someone else? Ever try to do something special for one in need? You did it to Jesus. If you joyfully received a little one, you received Jesus.

He said, "Whoever receives one such child in my name receives me, and whoever receives me, receives not me but him who sent me."

The next time you are even a little bit thirsty, on a mountain or not, I hope you will think of how you can serve Jesus in a special way. There are lots of little ones, and even older people, around.

The Bible reading is in Matthew 25:34-45

I Started a Forest Fire

I used only one match.

I really didn't mean to, but this is how it happened.

It was years later when I again climbed Mount Aboro, this time as the dorm parent, the leader, the one responsible for all the kids who were climbing up with me. I was out to share some of the great memories from my time at Rethy, but we didn't plan to stay overnight on the mountain.

To make my fire, I used dry materials on a brilliant sunny day at noon unlike when I saw Mr. Stauffacher make his fire in the rain, at night, with wet wood.

When I started my fire, it was easy. We had climbed up the mountain with dust and pollen blowing in our faces. The moss beards that hung from the dead branches on the forest trees were now a dusty gray, instead of the usual light green. The grass rattled, rather than swished as we pushed our way through it avoiding the hard and sharp thorns the best we could. Even the leaves seemed to clatter against one another. It was extremely dry.

At the top of the mountain, the view was obscured in the dry season haze. Lake Albert couldn't even be seen. All the puddles that were normally in the rocky depressions were gone. The mud at the bottom of each had dried up and cracked into small cubes. Thin tan flakes curled up in the hot sunshine where the edge of the pool had been. The small aloe cactuses were the only plants that still looked alive. It was hot. It wasn't hard to start the fire.

For some reason the kids wanted some hot tea to go with their sandwiches. It is possible that I offered the idea. Their sandwiches were all wadded up in the bottom of the plastic bags they carried; the peanut butter and jelly blended into the bread. Dust and bits of dry leaves and a few insects had somehow gotten into the bags, but the kids thought they would like some hot tea. Sure, I'll be glad to make a fire. I didn't think.

I didn't need to worry about kindling; plenty of dry grass lay all around. The twigs easily snapped off the branches of the small dried, dead, bushes. It wouldn't take long to make a hot fire. The kids helped gather what we needed, well, maybe a bit more than we needed, but plenty to get a good fire started. I used only one match.

The fire caught hold immediately. Soon it was crackling cheerfully among the rocks in the sheltered hollow we had selected. Then a gentle breeze began to blow. It felt so good. In the stifling stillness, our sweat wouldn't even evaporate in spite of the baking heat. The breeze picked up and so did the fire.

A tall clump of lemon grass at a small distance from the fire, between a couple rocks, suddenly burst into flames. We tried to stamp it out, but burning curls of grass floated upward from beneath our feet. The wind carried them a short distance and they drifted back down to settle on more clumps of grass, which also began burning almost immediately.

By now many of us were trying to stamp out the fires, trying to beat them out with little dry bushes we pulled up, only to find new fires starting yards away, and our little bushes catching on fire. The twisting spinning bits of burning grass and sparks drifted ever higher and further away, as the heat from the increasing number of fires became ever more intense. I had started a fire all of us couldn't stop. We were forced to retreat from the heat and the growing orange flames. Back on the bare rocks, a few yards away, we could do nothing but watch and eat the wads of sandwich, without any hot tea.

There was no time to make kites, though the wind was perfect. With the fire now beginning to roar and spread rapidly, I collected everybody as quickly as possible, checked to be sure everyone found their partner, and we hurriedly began our hike back down the mountain. Had we waited much longer, the fire would have blocked our return path through the forest. The fire became so hot that there was surprisingly little smoke, yet we could clearly see the cloud of drifting sparks and ash towering above the mountain as we looked up behind us on our way back down the mountain.

That Saturday night, viewed from Rethy, miles away, the fire on the mountain proved to be a spectacular sight. Bursts of orange flames leapt up into the black sky every time another large tree was consumed like a brilliant torch. A huge circle of dancing, orange light around a black center, the fire burned its way down the mountain. There was absolutely nothing that could be done; no fire fighters, no government authority to phone, nothing could stop what I had started. I had started a forest fire with a single match.

Early Sunday morning, even from that distance, I could see that the mountain still burned, though only in small patches here and there. Mostly black, the mountain breathed isolated plumes of white smoke that drifted nearly straight up into the air. The wind must have shifted in the night and the fire had died down, at least as far as I could see. My single match had caused that tremendous black blotch on the mountain.

Shortly after I returned into the dorm, a man knocked at the door. Bleary eyed, tired, and none too clean, he apparently hadn't slept much that night. Clearly he had been drinking something much stronger than water and not fighting the fire, though he smelled of smoke. "I am the Agrinome," he stated, "I have heard that you were up on the mountain with your children yesterday. The chief has eaten a goat with the elders."

I realized that the celebrations had already begun. The celebration expenses were no doubt on credit, knowing that the muzungu had lots of money. He told me I was to report to the Zone Agrinome near Buba, halfway to Djugu, near the Blukwa /Linga turnoff. I had committed a serious "Infraction." Clearly, I was in trouble with the local forester from my single match.

After Sunday School that morning, I collected all the older boys, and we climbed into my blue Chevy four wheel drive pickup. We took old burlap sacks. We took hoes and shovels. We took axes, pangas, and my light blue Homelite chain saw. We were resolved to fight the fire and create a firebreak, so it could spread no further.

Well, by the time we arrived, we had a hard time deciding where to make a firebreak. The fire had burned itself out. It didn't seem to be heading anywhere and there was no wind. I guess all I can say is that the Lord made that fire go out.

We began hacking anyway, cutting a path near the only burning area we could find. The chain saw roared. Kids were hacking joyfully at the dry brush. They shoveled up dry dirt and tossed it into a bush, which was smoldering on the far side of the small area. Black dirt and flying ash soon has us looking a lot like the Agrinome who had been at my door that morning, at least in our complexion and the smell of smoke on our now filthy cloths. We really didn't do much good. The fire went out before we got our feeble firebreak completed.

Can a big fire come from a little match? It did! Was I very smart to light the fire on such a hot, dry, mountaintop without thinking of the possible results? Not very. Did I think before I lit a fire for some kids who would like some tea? Not at all. Was it easy to light the fire? Real easy. Can a big forest be burned, starting with a little spark? Yup.

The Bible calls the tongue a fire and tells us to consider what a great forest may be set on fire by a small spark. What is said may be evil, it may be wrong, it may be intended to hurt; it depends why we say what we do. What we say should be good and helpful to others.

How well do we control our tongues?

Lighting the fire was without forethought and very easy.

The Bible story is in James 3:1-10 & Ephesians 4:29

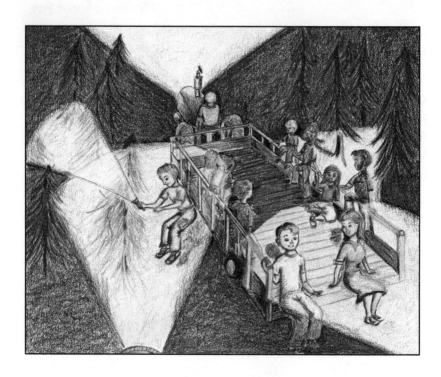

The Treasure Was Gold

A treasure hunt in the forest at night using flashlights, compasses, and measuring rods to find gold would make a good Saturday night activity. They might even learn a little about reading a compass, and orienting a map. As a dorm parent and teacher, I had signed up at staff meeting for a Saturday night activity for the whole school, and this would be a good one. We could take all the kids out to Camp Red Arrow in the six-meter trailer I had made to carry the power poles for the hydro project. I'd add a little hay and pull the trailer with the red and yellow Massy Harris tractor. The kids would have a great time! Ellen could give them hot cocoa when we came back while I was weighing in any gold they might find. I'd pay them ten Sengies a gram, measuring the weight of the gold with the pan balances from the science lab at school.

In my garage carpenter shop I prepared two identical thin rods, about 2 meters long. The two rods, a compass, a tape measure, a hammer, nails, and a pad and pencil were the items needed for our preparations in the forest. Dave, my fellow missionary and also a dorm parent, rode double out to the forest on my blue Yamaha 100 street bike. He held the long rods with one hand and somehow held on to the bike and me with the other. The long measuring rods projected out in front of us over the headlight while the hammer and nails were strapped to the carrier behind us with a strip of inner-tube rubber. The pad and pencil rested safely in my back pocket.

We arrived somewhere near where Mr. Miller had made Camp Red Arrow many years ago. When we stopped at the bridge, I discovered I now had two pencils and neither had a point. My red Swiss Army knife was always in my pocket so I had soon sharpened both pencil pieces. I pounded a nail in the log, which formed the curb at the edge of the small bridge. Standing on the log, over the nail, I selected a tree among the many straight trees some distance away.

Dave started measuring the distance to the tree with one of the rods, flipping it end over end, counting as he went. I sighted over the compass, lining up the two hair-lines and the tree. Holding the compass steady, I looked at the dial to read the number of degrees indicated on the dial. I recorded the number on my pad: 145 degrees. That is nearly south-south east. One hundred eighty degrees would be exactly south. I took my rod and began counting the number of rods it was to the tree. 23 rods, I counted. I stopped at the tree, pounded in a nail 2 feet above the ground. Since Dave had gotten the same distance, I wrote down 23 rods beside the 145 degrees. I could still see the log at the side of the bridge, so I sighted back to the bridge and got 215 degrees. The sum was 360 degrees, so my sighting checked. We selected another tree and repeated the process at a different angle and distance. We were mapping out a path through the dense, silent woods. The segments of different lengths, at different angles, made a crooked path towards a rocky hillside in the darkest part of the forest. That was where I planned to hide the treasure.

It was nearly noon by the time we had returned to the starting point and repeated the whole process making a second trail of similar length. The second trail started off in a different direction but zigzagged back to the same ending point. We walked back to the motorcycle and returned to the dorm for lunch.

The yellow enamel paint wasn't quite dry on the quartz rocks I had painted, but that didn't matter much. The dirt and pine needles that would cling to the strips of paint would make the 'gold ore' more authentic looking. I put the rocks in a small plastic bucket and, carrying it in one hand, drove back out to the forest after dinner to hide the gold. Some marked rocks I just threw here and there, scattering them on the rocky hillside at the end of our two trails. Others were buried; some I left partially visible. I hid a couple of the biggest ones a number of yards away from the rest.

That afternoon, I created two treasure maps, drawing the separate routes out to the approximate scale, using a ruler and a protractor. After rubbing some juice from a split lemon on the paper and scorching the edges of the parchments, I rolled the paper into two scrolls. I now had the ancient treasure maps all ready.

When we chose the teams after supper, there was lots of excitement. Biggies who knew how to use a compass were included on each team. They were given the treasure maps and the measuring rods. Kids went to get their flashlights and wanted us to open the canteen to buy new batteries.

The cold, starry night seemed particularly dark since the moon, which had been full just a couple of days ago, hadn't yet risen. The girls sang songs riding on the tractor wagon while the guys jumped off, ran through the bushes, and then came running up behind to climb on again. Flashlights bobbed here and there as we drove slowly down the airstrip, traveling parallel to the road that led to the forest. At the end of the strip, I had everyone get in.

The moon was just starting to rise when we got to the bridge. I shown my flashlight on the nail and explained the rules again.

"The gold is in rocks similar to this one which I dug up in the area at the end of your treasure maps," I said. "The treasure maps look to be similar to the one I lost. Follow them carefully and seek for the gold, even if your team doesn't get there first. Keep the gold you find, and I'll buy it at 10 Sengies a gram when we get home tonight."

Chattering together, the kids tried to decide what to do. First, they studied the maps, and finally one team shown their brightest flashlight over the compass along the bearing and began measuring off rods and counting.

The other team began to argue. "This is stupid," Danny said. He rotated the map and looked off towards the hill. "I know where the gold is anyway. I don't need this old map." He shoved it at Keith.

"Which way do we go?"

"I'll do the measuring; I'm older than you."

"Where is the compass?"

"Does it have to point north?" They shined their flashlights at the compass and in each other's eyes. They didn't ask for any help, though I was just standing there, wanting to be asked. Keith held the map, turning it first one way and then the other. I thought at least the picture of the road and bridge I had included in the map would help them to know the general direction of the first sighting. Danny wasn't interested in working as their leader, and I knew he could read the map. He had done so well in science class.

One of the kids grabbed the rod, trying to take it, apparently wanting to use it like a spear. "Gimmie that," yelled the first, and got a hold on the other end of the slender rod. It nearly snapped. No one else said anything. They just stood there.

From a distance off in the woods we heard the happy voice of some Titchie, "Hey, here is the nail, just like Pa Brown said." He had discovered the nail in the first tree. The guys measuring with the rod had almost gotten there. "Which way do we go now?" was the next thing I heard. Alan's team definitely had the idea.

Danny had disappeared. I went to help the other team. I knew Keith could lead the team, so I told the kids they could follow Keith. He could read the compass, I was certain, in spite of his thick glasses.

Keith took the compass, holding it directly in front of his chest and began to rotate. Stopping when he saw 145 under the sight marker on the opposite side of the little brass instrument, he shown a flashlight from his chest across the compass over the 145 and told the kids to go look for the tree with the nail in that direction.

"You guys measure the distance in the direction where I am shining my light. I'll stay here pointing the light. Don't stop until you count up to 23 rods, unless someone finds the nail first. If they don't find the nail before you get to 23, stay right there and we will all come there to look in the trees nearby." Keith had it. Off they went!

"Hey you guys, I already found it." The faint cry from off in the forest told of further progress by Alan's team.

It wasn't long before Keith's team found their first nail and disappeared into the forest in a different direction.

The nearly full moon had now risen, and the white light illuminated the road by the bridge where there were no overhanging trees. I started up the old tractor and turned on its one headlight, which had been fabricated from my old Yamaha headlight. It was necessary to drive down the road to an old intersection in order to be able to turn around the old Massy Harris tractor with the long wagon. I planned to park at the top of the hill not too far from where they should soon be searching for my concealed quartz rocks with the strip of yellow paint on the side.

It looked like the prospectors were already there! I could see where white and yellow beams from the flashlights stabbed the dark shadow under the trees. Beams of light flashed in every direction. Suddenly the indistinct, random, chatter was punctuated by a little girl's voice that I heard clearly, "Hey I found a big one!" The lights instantly lost their random sparkling as they converged towards one spot, blinking as each passed behind the dark tree trunks on the way there.

When I joined them, several kids brought their rocks for me to see. The rocks I had hidden had been found, some very small, but some filling their hands filthy from the search. The Titchies had done very well. Danny was there too, but he didn't come show me what he had found. "You should see Kathy Williams rock; it's huge! She got here the last of all of Danny's team, and she just picked it up!"

"I got two, look!" said another Titchie. One of the rocks in his hand did have the yellow paint, but the other was a piece of granite common in the forest on this hill.

"This one looks good," I said, "see the gold? I wonder if the essayer will find any gold in this one. We'll see."

I had everybody find their buddy, and we started back to the tractor and trailer. Danny cooperated too; he didn't feel like walking back to the dorm alone. It was getting cold; the moonlight was casting black shadows on the gray grass and the pale road. The area illuminated by the lone tractor headlight was usually in the bushes, but Ronnie shown the light from his flashlight on the road to help. It wasn't really necessary in the bright moonlight. The kids were unusually quiet, sitting low in the trailer, keeping warm. It had been a good treasure hunt.

The Titchies were even more eager to weigh their gold than to get the hot chocolate. They anticipated spending the money from the "essayer" at the canteen on their favorite candy. They had trustingly followed the beam of their captain's flashlight over his compass and looked for the trail marked by nails in the trees, just like he said. Now their gold, except unfortunately that piece of granite, turned into real money!

Danny had only one small rock to be weighed in the pan balances. I placed it in the left hand pan. I removed one of the brass weights and then two of the smallest brass weights in the right pan brought the pointer to the center, swinging first right, and then left two marks: fifteen grams. He grudgingly accepted his small pile of Sengies, equal to one and one half Makutas.

Selfishly thinking he would get the most if he got there first, he had gone his own way through the forest, but had ended up with less than most had just received.

"GOLD" IN THE PAN BALANCE

"There is a way that seems right to a man, but its end is the way to death." That proverb is repeated twice in the Bible, just in case we don't get it the first time.

There is only one way to God, the way God provided.

The Bible reading is in John14: 1-6

Other Nice Girls

Remember the little girl with the curly brown hair and the straight little nose that put me on top of the world? Her name was Myra Lou. Remember Peter who was apparently more dashing than I and by some means known to him got her to like _ _ _ _ _ so much? Would you like to know... the rest of the story?

A few months later, Peter found more excitement somewhere else; Myra wrote me a note. Her brother delivered it after study hall in the little open walkway between the dining hall and the boys' hall of our dorm. I sat on the low wall and read it by the light that came from the study hall windows. Mr. Stauffacher was still helping Mary Anne with her Geometry. I still remember part of it, "I wish we could be back on the old footing again," she wrote.

I wasn't sure what "the old footing" was from her point of view, but for me it had been in the clouds on top of the world! Lots had changed since then. I don't remember the rest of that little note, except that it was a nice note. She was really a special girl. I could tell by all the activities that were shared in dorm life; the way she did her work at school and how she did her dorm jobs, and how nice she was to her brother. You could tell a lot about her personality by the way she participated in the games and by her reaction when she had sold her lunch at the Box Social. The lunch tasted good, and she was fun to talk with.

Our family had even visited her family at their house because my parents were good friends with her parents. We went to Maitulu during one of the school vacation months. I had shot a Palm Nut Vulture from the air with my Dad's shotgun and remember skinning it out to stuff. The huge bird had lots of fat beneath its skin. The skin didn't come off nearly as easily as any of the other birds I had stuffed, and there was too much else to do. We hiked off a long ways and hunted monkeys in the jungle trees along the wet valley streams near the corn gardens. The people were keen to have us come because a troop of monkeys could destroy a crop in a short time. We swam in the cold, spring fed pool that they had dug down in the valley, in the shade of the gigantic forest trees not far from their house. I had observed how she interacted with her brother and her parents at home, but that was when she liked Peter. I spent most of the time with her brother. Unfortunately, I had to throw the Vulture skin down the outhouse hole since before I had skinned out the head, it had started to rot in the warm, humid tropical air.

I felt that I had been betrayed. She was the first girl I had ever noticed, but she had decided she liked _ _ _ _ _ instead of me. It was impossible to return to the innocent joys of Winkum, Fruit Basket Upset, and Pom-pom Pull-away. Maybe subconsciously I still thought of that worldly earring which actually turned out to be a bobby pin. We never did get back on the old footing; I haven't seen or heard from her since I left Rethy.

By the time her brother gave me that note I had found Nellie. She was a new girl who had recently come to Rethy, and she looked to me like one of those pretty young women in the Montgomery Ward Catalog. I'm sure they chose those girls to show how nicely a girl's dress can fit. She always looked like she had on a new dress. The narrow black stripes on her yellow dress flowed just right. She was very distracting when we played Ping Pong because girls don't hit the ball the same way guys do. She liked playing Ping Pong, so I would often check to see if she was playing; then join in the Round Robin game if she was there.

I remember being a little ashamed of what I saw on the palm of my hand when I was slapping the Ping Pong paddle against it, waiting for her serve. Here I was, totally mesmerized by her graceful serve, actually her, not the serve, when I saw the PHB+MLH in the heart at the base of my left index finger. I had cut the callous as deeply as I could, until it hurt, then filled the cuts in with blue ink from my ball point pen. A short time ago I had wanted it to last forever, but now I wanted it to go away. I had tried grinding it off on the rough edge of the cement cap on the low wall at the end of our hall, but the heart was still there. I had washed the dorm dishes for the whole week I was on the dish crew, but the hot water hadn't made it fade away. Now I hoped Nellie wouldn't see it.

Croquet was another game that became popular, and I tried to get in the game when Nellie was playing. The other guys couldn't help but notice her either, and I guess that was one reason we all raced to get the mallets after school. She sometimes just watched with the other girls. I guess we were a bit foolish, but I know I tried to play my best and stand just right when she was watching, hoping that she was cheering for me. I even combed my hair before I went to play.

Her younger brother, David, had come to Rethy the same time she did. He didn't have any friends at first, but he liked pets, so he soon became friends with others who had pet guinea pigs. I wasn't as interested in mine any more, especially since I had discovered girls, but I still had several and gave him some of them. I kept the mother with the three tiny ones. It was still fun to care for them. David used to follow me when I went out after dish crew to pick grass from the sorghum field before dark. Those guinea pigs ate a lot at night. They liked pigweed the most which grew best at the edge of the dorm garden. I didn't mind him tagging along. He might talk about his sister. I was a little amazed to discover that he thought of me as a Biggie; it seemed I would always be a Titchie. He said I had a barrel chest and was very strong. I kind'a liked hearing that. I guess he was still a Titchie for sure.

One day he did talk about his sister, but he didn't seem to want to. He started several times to say, "My sister...," but he didn't finish his sentence. Probably I looked foolishly eager, and he admired me too much to tell me what she told him to say. Finally he said, "My sister doesn't want you to be around so much," or something like that; and I got the idea. I suppose she thought Peter, or maybe Bruce, much more dashing. That night I picked so much sorghum and pigweed that my little guinea pigs had only eaten out tunnels to the front of the cage by morning.

Well, there were other new girls besides Nellie that also liked to play croquet. The grass had all been worn away in front of the wickets making a depression that could be used to one's advantage. If you calculated carefully, using the correct angle and hitting it just right, the ball would roll in an arc and hit the ball in the depression. I discovered Esther was a better sport than Nellie. She was a new girl too and loved to play croquet. She was an amazingly good shot, especially for a girl. I played lots of croquet with her.

I need to tell you a little about croquet. In the normal game, the nine wickets are set up in a pattern on the playing field between the two stakes. Play starts and finishes at one stake, progressing through each wicket to the far stake and back again. Each wicket must be passed through in a specified order and direction until the best player succeeds in completing the circuit. If everyone takes his turn and doesn't hit any other player's ball the best shot would win. Things aren't always predictable, however, since hitting each other's balls is allowed and introduces strategy including shipping.

Shipping an opponent's ball is one of the options available after hitting their ball. One can continue play with two extra turns, beginning from where their ball stops after striking the other ball. They can take two turns but start from any point the length of a mallet's head from the other ball. Or, they can place their ball next to the other and for the first extra turn hit their own, causing both balls to travel. When shipping Esther's ball, I would put my ball in contact with hers, align them to direct hers at a specific target, hold my ball with my toe, and strike my ball very hard. If I succeeded in shipping her ball through a wicket when she had gotten poison first, she would laugh and sort of swish her long skirt as she went to the starting post to challenge me to another game.

SHIPPING THE BALL

Esther was an excellent student and planned to be a nurse someday. She was the kind of girl I could talk with, and she made me feel like I had something to say, though I have no idea now what we talked about. Not very much really, but she would always smile back when I smiled at her. She liked to go to the Stauffacher's living room early, before our evening dorm devotions, look at magazines and listen to the classical music. I found that one National Geographic magazine article lasted a long time, since I spent more time looking at her, waiting for her to look up from her reading, than looking at the pictures of the Okapi in the Congo jungle, somewhere near Stanleyville. After a while, I guess everyone agreed that she was my girlfriend. Even Winkum got back some of its old joy. She was a faithful gal.

At graduation time from Rethy, I worked a long time on the poem I wrote in her yearbook. She wrote something sweet in my Rethy Rambler too. I don't remember any more what either of us wrote, but I do recall that I told her that my Esterbrook pen would always remind me of her. For a long time it did remind me of her, but we went our different ways after tenth grade at Rethy, and my pen has since disappeared. We lost touch, though later I learned that she had married Bruce. I was happy for both of them. I've since seen her and Bruce when I was a guest with your grandma in their home. She still looks much the same as she did when I first knew her, and she is a nurse specializing in some kind of heart examinations & treatment using slender probes that are fed up into the heart through the veins or arteries.

I heard that my first little girlfriend, the one that put me on top of the world, grew up, got married, and had children. I understand that she has also gotten rather heavy from some medical problem, but I've never seen her again and I don't even know her new name.

Whatever happened to Peter? He was at Wheaton College with me, and we roomed together our sophomore year. He was the mature collegian; he shaved daily. I tried to remember before ROTC inspection days since the sergeant was likely to say, "You need a shave, Cadet," when in fact it was doubtful. Peter even used Burma Shave from the fat little tube to rub on his head before he shaved off all of what little was left of his receding hair. I wished I had at least a little bit of a receding hairline and looked less like a kid. (Yule Brenner films were out then, I think, though I didn't see them until 25 years later. We had pledged not to go to the movies.)

I next saw Peter in his dark home full of heavy rich mahogany furniture. He had married a beautiful girl I had admired in college because she had beautiful, waist length, soft hair. (I am not sure it was soft 'cause I never touched it, but it looked that way.) They kept their house dark because he had some kidney problem and light hurt his eyes because of the medication he took. He remarked that my wife looked like the kind I would choose. (She has soft hair... I know. She is very beautiful still.)

Denying his heritage and all he had learned as a missionary kid, Peter had converted to Mormonism. He gave me a Book of Mormon, so I could be enlightened. I didn't read his Book of Mormon. I'd rather walk in the Light.

Next I heard that his mother had given him one of her kidneys, and he was doing much better. Later I saw him with a new wife, who had come complete with five children. I am not sure what happened to the girl with the long, soft (I think), brown hair, but they had had no children. A Mormon man, they say, can bring several wives into the Kingdom. So, was Peter doing his duty? Peter died before he was forty. He now knows "the Rest of the Story."

Is that all there was to life for Peter? I remember at Rethy being concerned lest the Lord come back before I was 21 years old. Somehow, that was the magic number. (I didn't get married until I was 25.)

Is the enjoyment of eating, drinking, marrying and giving in marriage all there is to life? That is what the people in Noah's day were doing, certainly ignoring the guy building an ocean going vessel and filling it with animals. Oh yeah, he preached for 120 years too. Of course nothing was going to happen. They had never seen rain. Any idiot who built such a boat hundreds of miles from water certainly wasn't to be taken seriously.

Life is ours to enjoy, so let's just live it. Nothing will change. They finally believed the warning when the flood swept them away.

They then knew the rest of the story.

The Bible reading is in 2 Peter 3:1-1-9

Alone, Back in Africa

When I go home
To my lonely room
And find there's no one there,
And then each time
I think of you,
Please answer, this one prayer
And give me, Someone,
To cry to,
Someone to say, "I do",
Someone to whisper, "I love you."

I was alone. I was watching the 5-inch reels on my German made Telfunken tape recorder, winding slowly round and round, as I listened to Jim Reeves softly singing words that expressed pretty well what I felt. Obviously, my memory is slipping as to the tune and the words, but I do remember the aloneness, lying diagonally across my bed thinking that everyone I knew and loved was far away.

When an MK leaves the boarding school that has been their home since first grade, when they leave the friends and even those they felt were enemies, there is an empty feeling. It is leaving all the life they have known. I left my family, my little sister, whom I barely knew, and headed off to college. Friends are the hardest to part with because you have the idea you will never see each other again. God is the only one who does not change and who always is there.

It was 1966. I had graduated from Wheaton College two years earlier. I was at Kagwe, not so far from RVA, back in Africa where I wanted to be, but things weren't what I had thought they would be.

I was the headmaster of a Kenyan Harambe high school, Gatamayu High School. I hardly found time to use The Jacado air rifle I had immediately purchased to replace the three guns Kenya Customs had confiscated. The specimens I had planned to collect for the Chicago Natural History Museum were still flying free. The gold-colored, four-wheel-drive International Scout with the removable white hard top, which I had imported with which to roam Africa, sat idle in the driveway. I was so far in debt from the shipping costs that I couldn't afford to run it and had no time anyway. I had all the headmaster responsibilities to care for as well as teaching the classes I had assigned to myself: Math, Science, and all the English classes.

This was not exactly what I had had in mind when coming back to Africa, and she was far away. All I had of her was her picture (I couldn't believe she was so beautiful), a steadily growing accumulation of blue air letters (I always wanted more, though we wrote daily), and on my little finger I wore her high school class ring.

Jim Reeves was singing;

"I don't want, a room full of roses,

I just want my arms, full of you".

I saved over 700 of her letters, which I now never read, but I have solved the problem that guy was singing about.

She had a ring from me too. I sold my Chrysler Imperial in order to buy it. As you might be able to guess from the size of the diamond, the Chrysler wasn't new, but I didn't plan to leave my attractive student nurse without some help to fend off all the doctors and interns at the West Suburban Hospital School of Nursing. I had also heard, somewhere, that the single lady missionaries might aggressively pursue a single male missionary, so I thought her class ring might be useful. They probably never even noticed me, but then I treasured that ring. I would never let her go. I would never lose that ring.

You know, there are values in your life that you probably accept right now as a young person, values that you should never let go; things that you should never compromise. You have a family who loves you, memories of your Christian upbringing that you should never be ashamed of, and friends who know you better than anybody, and love you anyway. Remember the story about tearing apart a little daisy? Loving one another is pretty basic. God made us in his image. He is Love. He is the one to whom you should hold fast. He is the one who changes not. The Lord your God is the one you should love with all your heart, with all your soul, with your entire mind, and with all your strength.

Well, I did lose that ring before I even left for Kenya. It was still sparkling and new. The blue stone set in gold glittered on the little finger of my left hand. It was too small for the finger I wanted to force it on, and slightly loose on that little finger. I planned to never take it off.

The shower in the basement of my folks' house, in Berrien Springs, Michigan, was really just a tin stall with a shower head, a couple of faucets on 1/2 inch pipe, a soap dish, and a great big open 1 and 1/4 inch drain. Oh yes, there was a plastic curtain too.

It was a good shower, until Ellen's ring dropped off, straight from my soapy hand down that drain. I immediately shut off the water. Forcing my hand down the drain was clearly impossible. It looked like it went on down forever into the dark under the concrete basement floor. There seemed to be no trap. Gold isn't attracted to a magnet. One doesn't have to be a Physics major to know that. I needed a very long skinny arm with a tiny hand at the end, and. . . . I had a little sister in sixth grade.

She was usually to be found in our big back yard after school, playing all by herself. She would run around and around in circles jumping over the low sticks she had set up at strategically selected sites. She ran with a peculiar kind of gate, which involved some sort of uneven leap after every two steps. Sometimes she would stop and briskly wipe her shoes on the grass, shaking her head from side to side, throwing her long, straight, blond hair from shoulder to shoulder. If it was windy enough, her long hair streamed behind her as she ran into the wind, her head tilted back. She was clearly "The Black Stallion" from Walter Farley's books. There was no faster horse that she would know of, well maybe she was a Palomino mare, but I favored my first guess.

That day I found her in the middle of a little circle of flowers, lifting her feet and slowly turning, well it was probably prancing with her head tipped to one side. I guessed she had won the race again, but that day I was more interested in her tiny hands and her skinny arm than her beautiful mane and her dusty, powerful hooves.

She actually seemed happy to be asked to come to help me. Maybe she even liked me. She eagerly came and slid her arm down that drainpipe, nearly to her shoulder. When she withdrew her arm I only saw Ellen's ring in her hand. Although thinking back, I am sure there was gray soap slime all the way up her skinny arm.

I can't recall ever thanking her, but I must have. I didn't know my little sister very well and have hardly gotten to know her since. How well do you know your siblings, your parents, and your family? I didn't do very well on that score. Even my favorite sister, Winnie, didn't get any letters from Kenya, nor did my parents. They would write Winnie to ask her roommate, Ellen, what I was doing. She was the only one who mattered to me and got written to every day, or even more often.

Please don't forget your family when you leave them to move out on your own. They will love to hear from you and they will certainly pray for you.

Remember the son who left home and went off into a far country and lived it up as long as the money he got from his father lasted? It wasn't until he found himself all alone, except for the pigs, and nearly starved, that he thought of his family. It appeared to his father that he was lost and dead, yet he still watched and waited.

What will it take to make you remember those in your family who love you, especially God who loves you with an everlasting love and continues to be kind to you drawing you to Himself.

I needed to lose the ring I highly valued before I thought of my need of my little sister.

The Bible reading is in Luke 15:13-32

Lost Near Kijabe

The second time I lost that ring, I lost it at Kijabe. I had ridden my bicycle through the forest from Kagwe to visit my friend, Norm Dillworth, at RVA. I could only afford to wash and wax that International Scout, so it sat there at Kagwe. I used the Raleigh Bicycle. Norm and I stayed in the small truck back camper, which was his apartment as the dorm parent for Westervelt Dorm. The dorm housed over forty high school boys and was then located where the wood shop, fish pond, and Science building are now.

That afternoon, I decided to go for a walk along the train tracks, so I hiked up past what was then Doc Propst's house taking a short cut up to the railway before reaching the tunnel. I headed left towards Kijabe town, walking on the shiny rails, counting my steps to see if I could get past my previous record without falling off. The bushes shook as some startled Colobus monkeys abruptly left their berry picking and swung up into the trees to check on my intrusion. They carefully peered around the tree trunk like curious old men, their white bearded, black faces, partly hidden. They didn't seem to realize that their flowing cape and the white plume on their tails made them contrast beautifully with the dark forest foliage behind them. I looked at the shining ribbon of rails curving ahead of me and around the next corner into the third ravine. Mount Longanot stood sharp and clear; the crater was dark, and the irregularities made black shadows on the hillside. The valley was green after the abundant rains. Only in Africa are the skies so blue! I bent and picked a tiny crimson flower to add to the ones in my shirt pocket. I planned to share my walk with Ellen and enclose some wild flowers. Thinking of her made everything so much more beautiful!

The stream that then went by the old watering station was rushing and gurgling as it disappeared into the tunnel under the tracks. I decided to follow it downstream but didn't go through the tunnel. I enjoyed making my own path through the brush. Even the tearing of the thorns was part of the Africa I had missed so much while in college. A Ross's Turacco suddenly flew off; its bright yellow beak and the deep red plumage on his head was a stark contrast to the dark iridescent purple of the rest of the bird.

Sometimes, I found it impossible to break through the underbrush and walked in the streambed, stepping on the slippery rocks. I traversed a few splashing sets of rapids, but then I came to a series of small waterfalls. Going down the third one, I slipped on the black rocks, catching my backward fall with my hands in the icy water. I was only partly soaked. One of my little flowers floated off downstream, a tiny crimson dot swirling in the foam. It vanished under the bushes a few feet ahead of me. I listened. Even the birds were temporarily quiet... I heard the sound of splashing water somewhere far below. I was at the edge of a cliff.

That proved to be as far as I could possibly go, so I headed back to RVA. It was already late. That night, while I was washing my hands for supper, I had a hollow empty feeling when I saw that the little blue and gold class ring was gone. I had again lost something I had promised to keep: lost it somewhere on that several mile hike while I had been so absorbed in enjoying the beauties of Africa. Maybe it was lost in the streambed where I had fallen backwards on those slippery black rocks at the top of the waterfall.

Of course I was out to look the next morning as soon as I could see. I hardly greeted the people I met. I got out of the way of the noisy, smelly train laboring up the hill, not even bothering to count the cars. My eyes were directed downwards, looking in vain for a little gold and blue ring. I found nothing. When I started down along the stream through the undergrowth, I realized that I could easily have lost it pushing the brush and thorns aside. Finding it could be impossible, but I was praying that it would be where I had fallen. Maybe it had followed the little crimson flower over the cliff during the rain that night. I found myself praying rather helplessly. Maybe God cared, even a little...

While enjoying my hike and looking at all that God had created, I hadn't been nearly as conscious of my need for Him as I was now that I had nearly given up hope of finding that ring again. Do we get so the creation God has made causes us to lose sight of the need for a personal relationship with our Creator. Would God understand my silly, simple prayer to help me find the lost ring Ellen had given me?

He did. It was there, glittering in a crystal clear pool of water, gently being rocked by the current, tiny bubbles growing and spinning by on their way over the falls. It could so easily have been washed away after the rain that had swollen the little stream. My "thank you" was sincere as I picked up the found ring and put it back on.

God cares about you. He gave me a heritage in Africa that is priceless and will always be part of me. If you have a similar heritage, accept it, enjoy it, and when tempted to hide it so you will better "fit in," don't. Rather, remember that your spiritual heritage is the only one that lasts, and this world is just temporary.

Value and hold on to what really lasts. All that God has so richly given us in this beautiful world He has made will pass away, even those we love the most. The meaning of life is that we might know him, love Him, and live.

Why give up what will last forever to gain something you cannot keep beyond this life?

Even so, I was glad to have again found my small gold ring with its slightly chipped blue stone.

The Bible reading is in Romans 1:16-23

Hold Fast to the Eternal

It was nearly two years before I lost that ring, again. The blue stone had become scratched and the corners chipped. I had nearly polished away the Lexington Christian High School emblem, but in my eyes, the ring sparkled as brightly as ever. By now there were over 500 blue air-letters hidden in my old battered suitcase with the rope handle. The transport and customs duty on my International Scout was finally paid. I knew because the Kenya Field Treasurer deposited way more money into my account than ever before. I could finally afford more than food, air forms, and stamps. I had even taken a month's trip to my home in Congo to visit my parents. I found thirty blue letters in my mailbox in Kiambu when I got back to Kenya. I had an even bigger pile to mail to her.

When I lost that ring this time, I was on a trip through the Seringetti plains with my friend Norm Dillworth. Game viewing by MKs is rather different from that experienced by tourists ...seated in rows, ...in the little white vans, ...with Zebra stripes painted on the side, recording everything with their Nikon, Cannon, or Exacta. MKs take pictures too, but the enhanced visual exposure they get results from a much more interactive experience. Proper game viewing requires initiative and a certain relationship with the animals.

The speed of a running ostrich can be maintained at nearly 35 miles an hour for over 2.5 minutes. He really wanted to cross the road ahead of us. The International Scout easily won.

Running Zebra are a little frustrating. When we chased them, they ran in great circles over rough ground and then stopped to watch. When we got near them again, they just ran again, stopping once again to watch us bounce ever nearer. With all those stripes on their faces it was hard to tell if they were laughing. I suspect they were. I guess they have superior equipment for their terrain. In the International Scout, we reluctantly gave up.

A hyena, carrying what must have been the femur of an Eland in his mouth, seemed ungainly and slow enough to run down with the Scout. His back legs appeared to be way too weak to make him move very fast, the bone too large to carry, his center of gravity far enough forward that he just might fall on his head, so we gave chase. He was, however, able to avoid our attack by turning in ever-smaller circles, out maneuvering the Scout, which was hampered by its large turning radius and its driver. The hyena must have felt cornered as we herded him round and round because he finally dropped his bone and changed direction, leaving at an angle perpendicular to the tangent of the circle at the point of decision.

The black leopard that leaped across the road in front of us also took an unfair advantage of the Scout when he ducked into a deep drainage ditch and disappeared. Fortunately, violent breaking kept us from following him into the ditch. Interactive game viewing was a great delight to us two MKs, at home in Kenya, laughing together, even though Norm had the nerve to ask why I braked so hard that he missed his picture.

After a while, the stimulus to interact with the animals was insufficient to draw us off the road. We had seen everything, except elephant. The dusty miles accumulated behind us on our way to Mwanza. The long-range gas tank was drained. The second tank registered nearly empty, the needle on the gauge quivering under the "E." It was hot, late in the afternoon.

"There's one," Norm said.

"Where?" I said.

"There," he said, his arm blocking my view forward, his finger pointing out my window. Sure enough, there was a black dot in the shade of the only huge, green tree to be seen anywhere. The stimulus to interact with the elephant was way beyond the resistance of two MKs with a four-wheel drive International Scout, even though the elephant didn't look big enough to fool with.

He was big enough. He was huge! Norm took a picture with my Exacta through the 400-millimeter lens. He took several with his Pentax. We were still a safe distance away and the interaction *could* be made more interesting. We decided the situation needed a little initiative and certainly a closer relationship with this great impassive beast. Maybe we could get a little action if we reduced the "inter-space" a little.

The Scout was good at brush barging, and when we came out again into the open, we had the elephant's attention. Norm took a few pictures with his camera, then a few with mine. He had the best view; I had the safest side of the car. The elephant settled down again.

I again took the initiative and roared the Scout's engine a couple times. Suddenly the urgency of getting into reverse was paramount. Coordination was gone. The engine that had roared a couple seconds ago, died. The Scout just jerked. It seemed intimidated. I was just plain scared. Norm was fumbling, looking for his camera, but fumbling.

The elephant came crashing directly towards us. Ears flapping, trumpeting loudly, his trunk extended. His quarry was a paralyzed driver, a stalled International Scout, and a photographer doomed to fail to record anything on film.

He dropped his trunk, stopped a short distance away, and then turned, disappearing into the brush. Norm's picture turned out to be a mass of gray with a blurred, indignant tail at the center. The elephant had taken the initiative from us.

Back on the road, monotony set in once again, I looked at the gas gauge needle that no longer quivered. I began pumping and releasing the gas pedal. Norm was instantly awake. "You're out of gas," he said. I just laughed, and poured on the steady power. We soon passed Norm's parents in their old blue Kombi.

All that was left of the trip was to race his folks to Mwanza. They were now just a cloud of dust a few miles behind us. The city was in sight. The Scout floated above the road as we took the washboard at the maximum possible speed that was consistent with turning corners. This was the life.

Suddenly the same symptoms I had simulated earlier reappeared. Norm seemed almost angry. "Don't fool around," he said.

"I'm not," was my helpless reply, as the motor died. We coasted to a stop, not three kilometers from Mwanza.

Speed was essential. We unlocked and heaved up the luggage cover. I grabbed the jerry tin filled with gas. The dust cloud chasing us could be seen to have a dot in front of it. The siphon hose was what we should have used, but slopping the gas through the small funnel we assumed would be faster. ...But it was slower and more wasteful it turned out. Now the dust billowed behind a faded blue Kombi, looming ever nearer. Norm's dad drew up alongside us just as I was shaking the gas off my hands. He leaned out, grinning through the swirling dust. "He who laughs last, laughs best," he chuckled. His pathetic little 1,200 cc VW engine screamed out its challenge, and the Kombi was soon hidden by its own red dust.

It took only seconds to re-pack and slam the luggage cover. It took many seconds, however, cranking the engine at full choke to draw in the fuel. Then we were roaring off down the washboard road, slewing around the corners, but we didn't catch up to the Kombi until we finally parked beside it under the Mango trees in the yard.

That night, in the shower before supper, I discovered my ring, her ring, was gone.

I had held on to that ring for nearly two years. It had become the emblem of my commitment to my fiancée. I had hardly thought of her at all that day and now even the ring was gone.

Perhaps you can't wait to "shake off" what you have seen as limiting your liberty. Maybe you want to hide your identity. Maybe you will try to blend into the new college culture or whatever environment you enter after leaving your Christian home. You may want to lose yourself and do everything that your parents won't let you do: life without a ring, life without God.

There is a postscript to the ring story. Lost between three and five kilometers from Mwanza on the main road, on a roadside path leading to the market, it would likely be found. It was dropped at about four in the afternoon and not missed until after dark. It would certainly be found. Not too likely I'd be the one to find it.

At daylight Norm and I set out. "It was about here," he said, so I stopped on the long stretch of straight road. There was not a landmark anywhere near. No way could he know exactly where it was. I could only remember on which side of the road we had stopped, the left side of course. I got out of the Scout, walked across the road, looked down, saw her ring at the edge of the path, and picked it up.

Two years, 1,400 letters, and two weeks later she gave me another ring. The blue and gold ring lost its significance.

Since then we have lived and worked 30 years in and been twice evacuated from Zaire/Congo. Our home was totally looted the first time. We evacuated by air, taking next to nothing with us. Since we left through Mahagi by road the second time, we had a few suitcases of necessary clothing and included some recovered blue letters. We had again lost nearly everything we had.

The Bible says: "That which is seen is temporal, but that which is not seen is eternal." and "Hold fast to what you have that you lose not your eternal reward." Some things just aren't very important.

Where is that ring now? We found it in a cardboard K-Mart jewelry box Ellen left at our New York farmhouse over 45 years ago. That little external evidence of my commitment to my fiancée isn't nearly as important any as it used to be.

It's not hard to figure out why, is it?

The Bible reading is 2 Timothy 1:12-14
and Revelations 3:1-6

About the Author

In 1942 Paul Brown was born in Arizona on a Navaho Indian reservation where his father worked as a doctor before moving to the Belgian Congo. Most of his early memories are filled with his experiences in Africa, at home in Zandeland and at the boarding school he attended through 10th grade.

Living among the needy Zande people his father, Paul Hart, an unpaid skilled surgeon, set up a one-doctor hospital. Though they offered healing, his parents had a far greater message sharing the good news of John 3:16 with patients before and during surgery. His mom, Raunie, was a nurse who worked with her husband and trained national nurses for their general practice.

After graduation from Wheaton College, Paul returned to Africa to become the headmaster of Gatumaiyu High School in Kenya. Two years later he came back to the States to marry his fiancé, Ellen Bearce and in 1968 the couple went to Rethy Academy to begin their years of service in the Democratic Republic of Congo. For over 30 years Pa and Ma Brown, as they are still affectionately known, taught, loved, and guided children in the very same boarding school where these stories took place.

Paul and Ellen now live on a small farm in Central New York where Grandpa tries farming. They serve in the local church and are seeking to use the gifts and heritage God has given them to show God's love to those He has prepared. The gift God offers is without measure, and cannot be earned yet leads to a relationship with Him that lasts forever.

Paul Henry Brown passes on this rich heritage to his growing grandchildren through his actions, words, and stories, some of which are written here.